The Teacher as Facilitator

by

**Joe Wittmer, Ph.D. and
Robert D. Myrick, Ph.D.**
University of Florida

Copyright © 1989
Educational Media Corporation®
Library of Congress Catalog Card No. 89-80322
ISBN 0-932796-27-3

Printing (Last Digit)
9 8 7 6 5 4 3 2 1

Publisher—

**Educational Media Corporation®
P.O. Box 21311
Minneapolis, MN 55421**

Production editor—

Don L. Sorenson

Graphic design—

Earl Sorenson

Dedication

To Diane Wittmer Thompson and Mark DeWayne Myrick
caring facilitative teachers

Table of Contents

The Authors...

Joe Wittmer, Ph.D. and **Robert D. Myrick, Ph.D.** are professors of counselor education at the University of Florida in Gainesville.

Preface

Many of our nations's leaders are calling for a complete restructuring of the public schools. They are alarmed at the number of students who fail to graduate and who lack the entry-level skills required by modern industry and technology. They recognize that our nation is at risk because so many young people are failing, misbehaving, and turning away from education. A nation at risk will be saved only by a nation of facilitative teachers who understand and value the process of learning.

Restructuring involves more than tinkering with the school curriculum, the size of classes, the updating of textbooks, or new equipment. It is more than raising test scores or graduation requirements. Cosmetic changes in education are not enough. At the heart of the reform process is the nature and quality of classroom teaching which takes place.

Professional teachers understand the purpose of schooling and its implications on the social, economic, and political structure of our country. They continually expand their academic knowledge. They also work toward a greater understanding of how to facilitate the learning of their students. They believe that the secret of success in teaching is to inspire the desire for learning, to spark interest, and to guide ambition. This requires good methods as well as a thorough knowledge of subject matter.

Harvard economist Robert Reich believes that the challenge is "to provide our children not with more education, but rather with a different kind of education." There is a need for an educational approach which introduces them to high technology and high-tech creativity—an education that stresses experimentation, not just repetition and drill. Reich also emphasizes that the engine of American productivity is no longer fueled by an elite corps of managerial wizards. The new engine is collaboration—collaboration among workers at all levels. That kind of collaboration demands schools to place more emphasis on cooperation and communication.

Schools must make up for the deficiencies of some parents and families. Children from disadvantaged backgrounds are not going to achieve academic excellence without special considerations. Exhorting or scolding them, or issuing educational edicts is not going to work. Rather, education for excellence embraces such concepts as:

- attention to individual differences
- a focus on all aspects of development—personal, social, emotional, and cognitive
- an integrated curriculum rather than isolated skill development
- active rather than passive learning
- small group instruction
- multicultural and nonsexist curriculum
- peer interaction and problem-solving

What are the strategies for reforming education? Many teachers are trained to work with the "ideal student" but often become demoralized when confronted those who are "at risk." Teaching is complex and there may be no single best way to do it. There are no correct techniques. Yet, there are some concepts and ideas, basic methods and strategies, which have proven effective time and time again. They have stood the test of time and they are the essential ingredients of the facilitative model of teaching.

JW
RDM

Chapter 1

The Facilitative Teacher
In the Classroom

Carl Willis, a 16 year-old dropout, was convicted at age 18 and sentenced to ten years in prison for armed robbery and selling illegal drugs. Although he is above-average in intelligence, his teachers labeled him as a brooding troublemaker who seldom did his schoolwork. His record indicated that he did well in school until the fifth grade, after which he did his schoolwork sporadically. He was often in difficulties with his teachers. In the seventh grade he was suspended from school twice for fighting. During the eighth grade he was suspended for swearing at a teacher. He once completed a written assignment in English entitled: Me, School and Life. The following is an excerpt from his paper:

> *I love the summer more than the winter which tells you something about me and school. I used to like school. Now, I hate getting up in the morning and thinking about school. Here at school I'm a nobody that gets yelled at by teachers. Here I'm not supposed to think for myself. I have to do what teachers say is good for me. But, I don't....*

> *After about a half day at school I'm tired and I feel about 90 years old.... I'm always looking for that last bell so I can get away from here.*

> *I don't know when I started hating school, but it seems like it was a long time ago. I'll never forget the second grade. One day I was playing with my pencil and it fell on the floor. The teacher screamed at me and hit me across the fingers with a ruler. When I was in the third grade the teacher made me sit in the hall with a sign on with the words "BAD EXAMPLE" because I was throwing dirt at some guys. The principal came down the hall and said I was a problem and never listened to anybody.*

> *I've been made to do everything in school from standing in a wastebasket to writing "I'm sorry" a 1000 times. There are a lot more things I could write about that I don't like. Would you like school if people there didn't like you?*

Did Carl Willis fail alone or did the educational process fail Carl Willis? School is supposed to provide life experiences in a microcosm for all students. What was Carl Willis' world like? What caused him to change his feelings about school, about teachers, about himself? It would be easy to attribute Carl's failure to his family, socioeconomic background, or other such peripheral considerations. But this draws attention away from school personnel and their responsibilities for meeting student needs. A common rationalization used by many educators in defense of their own failures is that the high risk students did not have a chance in the first place because of their unfortunate background or circumstances in life. Actually, school may have been their only chance and the best of circumstances.

Responding to Carl Willis

Assume that Carl Willis is still in school and is a student in your class. You want to help! You want to make a difference! You are the team teaching leader and Carl has been sent to you because the quality of his school work has dropped. It is apparent that he doesn't like school. He says to you:

> *Why do you want to talk to me? I know I said I don't like school, but I haven't done anything wrong.... Besides, I'm trying to get my work done. And that's what you want to get after me for, isn't it?....*

What would you say to Carl Willis in this situation? Write your response below (or on a piece of paper) before reading any further.

> *Carl, you...*

Imagine that on another occasion you are drawing attention to some errors in his homework. You are with a small group of students including Carl. He reacts by saying:

> *Everything I do is wrong. (His eyes water a little). I just don't do anything right. All the other kids hear you talk about me and they joke about it. Because of you, nobody likes me... I'm so dumb, and you, you... always find my mistakes... and tell everybody. (Tears come to his eyes).*

What is your response?

> *Carl....*

One day Carl says:

> *I wish I weren't in school. Sometimes it's okay, but most of the time I hate being here....(pause) But, it is better than staying home and being "nagged." This place (school)... they expect so much. Things would be great if I could get away from here... anything is better than this.... I don't know.... I might just quit....*

What would you say?

> *Carl....*

Do you think your responses would have encouraged Carl to talk more with you? Would they have helped Carl to understand himself better? This book focuses on interpersonal communication and student/teacher relationships. It describes what is, as well as where, when, and how to be, a facilitative teacher. Carl Willis needed some facilitative teachers in his life to help him with his academic progress and his personal growth.

Facilitating Academic and Personal Growth

All human beings have the basic need to strive toward physiological and psychological fulfillment. Unless it is thwarted, this drive for fulfillment and self-enhancement continually moves us toward physical and mental growth. Our reactions and their consequences to our various environments are incorporated into ourselves. When we encounter forces which cause us to become closed to our experiences, or doubt ourselves and those around us, our learning and personal functioning are impeded. This implies that one goal of education is to facilitate an open attitude about learning and growth experiences. It also implies that we must become more aware of our humanness and how it affects all our choices and decisions.

Just as our body has an internal self-healing process, it also has a drive for personal growth. Some theorists refer to this process as a search for self-fulfillment. Others describe it as a need for the maintenance and enhancement of self; or as a need for self-actualization; and as a process of becoming (Purkey & Novak, 1988). Although most teachers want to facilitate the personal growth of their students, in too many cases, they are hampered by traditional and conventional approaches. Ineffective approaches are detrimental to student learning and they make teachers' work too difficult, if not impossible.

A great number of school environments are not facilitative of positive personal growth. For example, nearly one million youths drop out of school each year, seeking personal meaning elsewhere. In addition, thousands of students each year fail to be promoted to the next grade level.

Escapism through drug abuse continues to be a national problem and it has taken its toll on our youth. Schools cannot be blamed totally for the increase in the use of illicit drugs; however, a young person attends school almost 1,000 hours a year and certainly school plays a large part in helping individuals learn ways of coping with stress and social problems.

Our society has not always encouraged the expression of feelings, especially as part of the learning process. In too many instances, feelings and emotions are seldom recognized in the classroom. Students who are not allowed to tune into their feelings in school may turn on to drugs after school.

Cheating appears to be widespread among students, both those who are attaining high grades and those who are not. What is it about the educational process that encourages young people to be dishonest with themselves and others?

School vandalism and violence have increased over the years and there is some evidence that it may be in direct response to the reputation of school personnel. Mayer and Butterworth, in their classic study on violence in the schools (1980), concluded that school personnel contribute to the problem because of their attitudes and behaviors. Ironically, educators seem to perpetuate the very violence and vandalism of which they are victims.

Is it getting any better? According to a widely read report in *Time Magazine* (February, 1988), things may be getting worse:

> *The dire condition of the nation's urban school systems is by now a familiar story, but some hard facts and illuminating incidents bear telling:*

- *In Detroit, high school dropout rates are 41%, with 80% in the worst inner-city districts.*

- *In St. Louis, 1 of 4 girls in pubic schools becomes pregnant before reaching her senior year.*

- *In Boston schools last year, 55 students were expelled for carrying guns and 2,500 must report to police probation officers for past offenses.*

- *In Chicago, an open house for the parents of 1,000 pupils at Sherman School drew five mothers and fathers.*

- *In Texas, the 100 top-ranked school districts spend an average of $5,500 a year per child, while the bottom 100 spend only $1,800. The results are evident in San Antonio's Edgewood district, one of the state's poorest, where 50% of students fall below the national norms in reading and writing.*

- *In Philadelphia, an administrator describes conditions at an inner-city school: "People coming to class high, not just pupils but teachers as well; filthy bathrooms; gang intimidation; nowhere to hang coats without them being stolen."*

- *In New York two weeks ago, Principal Edward Morris asked for a transfer from Park West High, where he had clearly lost control of violence-prone students, and where students in the cafeteria stomped a girl so brutally they broke her ribs.*

The report continues:

> *In many schools these realities blend into a pattern of horrors for teachers and administrators. Odette Dunn Harris, principal of William Penn High School in Philadelphia, talked of confiscating crack bags from student pushers in a neighborhood torn by gang wars and racial strife. When she first arrived at the school..., "They had riots in the lunchroom. The fire gong used to go off every five minutes, and that was the cue for the kids to break out." Some youngsters still carry knives and guns as casually as pocket combs. One parent assaulted her, and she noted, "I've had kids say to me, 'I'm going to punch you,' or they call me 'that bald-headed bitch' because of my short hair."*

> *At Principal McKenna's Washington Preparatory High in Los Angeles..., three female students, about to cross the street to enter the schoolyard, were wounded in the sudden cross fire of a gang ambush. Says McKenna: "I personally buried six young men last year who had gone to this school, and I do the same thing year after year" (Time, p. 54, 1988).*

Many young people are depressed and schools may be a contributing factor. The rate of suicide among young people has increased rapidly. Statistics suggest that most college and high school students who committed suicide had normal or superior intelligence but were performing poorly in school. The proportion of school-aged people seeking psychiatric assistance has also increased dramatically over the past few years. School discipline, according to public polls (1988), is still the number one concern of teachers, administrators, parents, and even students.

No matter then what microscope one uses to examine schools, it is clear that many schools are not doing all that they could and should do. Such problems may seem insurmountable, but they can be lessened—their life-ruining dimensions diminished—if teachers view themselves as facilitators of academic and personal growth.

Facilitating Student Learning

A teacher committed to facilitating students will provide learning situations where learning is:

1. Personally meaningful

2. Postive and non-threatening

3. Self-initiated

4. Self-evaluated

5. Feeling-focused.

Learning is Personally Meaningful

Methods of learning can be placed along a continuum. At one end is *didactic* learning, where emphasis is placed on talking and the use of verbal and nonverbal symbols to conceptualize meaning. This usually involves listening to another person's ideas, memorizing, and feeding back the material that was presented. Too often a teacher, or another authority figure, selects what is to be studied and discussed, many times without regard for its personal meaning for the learner. When it evokes little feeling or emotion in a student—no special personal meaning—it has little relevance. There is, perhaps at best, a small measure of academic progress. It may even hinder personal growth.

At the other end of the continuum is *experiential* learning. This type of learning has the quality of personal involvement. Consequently, it is more significant and meaningful. Through experiential learning, knowledge is gained primarily from one's own actions, practices, and perceptions. In other words, learning is acquired through having an experience and talking about that experience.

Because significant learning occurs when subject matter is seen as having relevance for one's own purposes, it is important to discover students' perceptions and the unique impact it has on thinking and feeling. For instance, two students taking the same course may perceive concepts presented in a lecture very differently. Only when they are asked to share their thoughts and feelings can the full effect of the lecture be revealed.

Standing behind a lectern and imparting information in an enthusiastic manner will not assure that the material is going to become a part of the student's knowledge base and self-system. It is probably incorporated only if the presented information has personal meaning for the listener. However, when experiential learning also takes place with the same material, then the element of personal meaning is built into the experience and learning is likely to be enhanced.

This does not mean that factual knowledge is less important than personal meaning. Factual knowledge is needed in order to acquire a mastery of certain concepts, to learn reasoning processes, and to solve everyday problems more efficiently. It provides us with a base of information from which to organize our thoughts and to have reactions. Moreover, learning need not always feature the learner actively doing something. Learning by doing is a popular principle of modern education that was first emphasized by the educational philosopher, John Dewey. Yet, there is little doubt that when students come into direct contact with practical problems, whether they be social, ethical, or otherwise, more personal learning takes place. Active learning is simply more powerful than passive learning. Learning by doing, unfortunately for most of today's students, means that teachers "do" while students observe and listen. Students can learn important concepts which influence their lives through watching a film, listening to a lecture, or reading a book. The central questions are: How relevant is it to the learner? Can learners discover personal meaning for them in the knowledge that they have?

If schools are to provide valuable learning experiences, then the curriculum must deal with issues and questions that students feel are relevant to them. If we are to facilitate personal growth in students, then we must be willing and able to hear their questions:

- *Why do I have to hide certain parts of my body and let others show?*

- *Why do I get in trouble so much of the time?*

- *Why do they bury people under the ground?*

- *Why should I have to act like an adult?*

- *Why is it wrong to hit someone, if that person hits me first?*

- *Why does school have to be more work than fun?*

Mastering the process of learning is a modern concept. Recognizing that learning is a process which requires an openness to experience and personal involvement is an important first step to helping students learn more effectively and efficiently.

Change is inevitable and learning why and how to change is invaluable. If society is to survive and to progress, it must have individuals who recognize change as a central part of life and accept that fact. Society also needs individuals who view learning as a change process that is continuous and meaningful. Change can be for better or for worse, and it is knowing and managing the learning process that makes the difference.

Learning Is Positive and Non-threatening

There are several myths in education that have been perpetuated over the years. Perhaps one of the most devastating is the proposition that children do not like to learn; that is, they must be forced to learn. The word *forced* may seem harsh. But, a study of practices suggests that many teachers see learning as generally unpleasant and hard work for students. It is, therefore, the teacher's job to push and pull in order to help them learn.

Actually, it is unrealistic and a near impossible task to force someone to learn. Resistance can be so firm that the lesson learned is one that is different from the one to be taught. Forceful threats, coupled with ineffective teaching skills, often masks the learning of some inappropriate things of which teachers are unaware. A stern and demanding history teacher may think that one is teaching the love and value of history when, in fact, students are finding it boring, uninspiring, and meaningless. Instead of appreciation and opening their eyes to history, students might deny, distort, or form a tunnel through which they narrowly interpret what is being presented. What is really being learned?

Students want to do things that are personally fulfilling and self-enhancing. A facilitative teacher knows that threats or the use of gimmicks to motivate students are of limited value. Rather, the facilitative teacher helps to nourish the desire to learn that is a natural part of all human beings. This means finding a way to get students personally involved with whatever is being presented or studied. It is centering the learning process on the student.

Any kind of threat tends to make individuals withdraw or fight back. Some teachers respond by developing elaborate sets of rules and then forcing students to comply with rules in the hope that there will be less need for discipline and fewer conflicts. In fact, such conditions usually create conflict. Some teachers strike out physically or verbally at students who do not follow their rules or directions. Teachers who are classroom management centered, rather than student centered, often find themselves at odds with students and too much of their time is devoted to disciplining and enforcing rules than to fostering learning.

One of the authors was visiting in a fourth grade classroom when the teacher called on a girl to answer a question. Jimmy, an enthusiastic and impulsive boy, blurted out the answer first. The teacher looked at him coldly and remarked, "I said Mary. Are you a little girl, Jimmy?" The other fourth graders giggled and the boy was embarrassed. He remained quiet for the rest of the period. What did Jimmy learn from this situation? Did he learn to raise his hand before talking? Did he learn that everyone gets a turn and to wait his turn, or to give others a chance to participate? Or, did he learn to be quiet in order to avoid ridicule? Did he learn that a mistake can cast doubt on his own identity and subject him to taunting or ridicule? Did he learn that school was pleasant or unpleasant?

How do you view the following incidents? A kindergarten girl finished sharing something before the class and the teacher says, "That was pretty good, considering you don't usually finish your work." The young child's smile fades and with eyes downcast, she takes her seat quietly. One teacher required a boy to stand in a waste paper basket for punishment because he had been running around the room too much. The child afterwards said, "She thinks I'm trash."

A third grade boy was told by a P.E. teacher to take a turn at bat and try to hit the ball in a baseball game. The boy said that he didn't like the game and said he would just strike out anyway. The teacher casually remarked in front of the class that the boy would never amount to anything if he didn't try and that he had a rotten attitude. Furthermore, if he didn't take his turn at bat he was going to get an F for the day and could go sit by himself in the bleachers on the far side of the field. Not only did the comments hurt and cause the boy to doubt himself personally, but they communicated that a teacher can be a punitive authoritarian when expectations and rules are not followed.

Another teacher asked a group of students to study quietly. They were told to read a section in the class textbook. The teacher stepped out of the room for a few minutes and when she returned, several class members were busy talking with one another while few others were at work. She was furious. She walked to the front of the room to gain the class' attention and then announced that everyone was to write answers to all of the questions at the end of the chapter. Unless the questions and answers were turned in the following day, a grade of F would be recorded for the day's work. There was a cold silence for the rest of the period. Students glared at each other and on occasion cast angry looks at the teacher when she wasn't looking. One wonders what that particular section of material in the text meant to those students. The teacher was able to force the students to comply with her need for silence, but what else did the students learn?

There are some teachers who pride themselves on being tough and talk of ways which discipline children when they are out of order. Some proudly pass their methods to others: "Copy 5 pages of the dictionary." "Write five hundred times the phrase: I will be a better person." "Don't smile at them for the first six weeks." "Load the work on them, so that they won't have time to fool around." Some have even erroneously concluded that they can pound (paddle) learning into children. There is a classic cartoon which shows a young boy spread across his teacher's lap. The teacher has a raised hand and is obviously getting ready to spank the boy. The caption is "I'll teach you to hit other children." With such a model, the child learned just that.

What kind of models do teachers provide children? Do they model that learning is fun and a vital part of the everyday process of living? Or, do they model that learning is unpleasant, tedious, unrewarding, and something to be avoided unless you have no other choice?

Regardless of what arguments educators use, in schools or classrooms where there are a lot of rules and policies, students sense that what is most desired is obedience and compliance. If students do not comply with the rules, usually determined by adults, they are typically described as troublemakers, goof-offs, incorrigibles, or potential dropouts.

In some schools noise is suspect because it is a violation of the unwritten rule that students learn best when they are quiet and busily reading and absorbing knowledge. There are still many schools where students sit in rows, facing the front of the classroom, and being quiet for most of the day. In order to maintain this "quiet study atmosphere," students learn that they must first obtain the teacher's permission before going to the library, to sharpen a pencil, to get a drink of water, to the bathroom, or to other classes. It is hard to imagine eighteen-year old seniors obtaining permission slips to go to the library when it is entirely possible that within a few months they will be studying on a college campus, entirely on their own, holding responsible jobs in local stores and factories.

The insistence on strict compliance causes conformity and impedes personal growth. Strict and rigid rules tend to limit the creative potential of students to think, feel, and respond independently.

You can probably remember examples from your own life where you experienced or witnessed teachers using punitive measures to force children to learn. Perhaps you can recall experiences when your own growth was thwarted, when learning lessons in school was something to be avoided. Do you remember any school rules that were responsible for your learning?

Do teachers seek obedience and compliance because they are afraid of what students might do? Do teachers doubt that students can be trusted to learn by themselves? Are they afraid that if students express themselves naturally and spontaneously nothing of value can be learned? Perhaps it is a combination of all these things, or maybe a failure of teachers to know methods which facilitate the natural desire to learn.

The authors of this book grew up in different parts of the country and went to different universities, but they both received the same advice as they entered teaching: "Be real tough on them for the first few weeks and then gradually ease up." The sad part is that it made some sense because it was assumed that students had a natural dislike for coming to school and that unless they were carefully corralled and guided into a learning situation, both teachers and students would fail.

Facilitative teachers do not hold the weapon of fear over the heads of their students. They know that students who are afraid of their teachers will see schools as unpleasant places to be. They know that fear closes doors to learning. They know that students can be emotionally crippled through the use of ridicule, sarcasm, and other methods that are used to gain conformity. They also know that playing the game of "going along with the teacher" is detrimental to the overall growth of their students.

In a revealing *Peanuts* cartoon, Lucy is sitting on a school bus with other classmates headed for a field trip in the woods. In the next to the last picture she says to herself, "Just maybe we won't have to line up to get off this stupid bus." In the last picture, however, she states simply, "No, it will never happen." For some teachers, rules exist because they always have been there. Some teachers are caught up in the trap of starting the school year with a list of rules that have been passed down to them, only to find out later they are unnecessary. Unfortunately, many of the things done in school and passed down through the years have been based on the assumption that students do not enjoy learning.

Teachers plan and structure learning experiences. This involves creating favorable conditions for learning, conditions that are appropriate for all the learners in the situation. This also includes the teacher. The critical question is: Are we trying to set up experiences to force students to think our way, learn our ways of behaving, or are the learning experiences constructed to help students think critically and to heighten their personal awareness?

When a classroom is characterized by threats and punitiveness, students learn they must conform if they are to get along with the teacher. Responsible independence and creativity are stifled because it is more important to find the answer deemed right by the teacher to avoid failure and punishment. Students learn to play the game. Some will give up and retreat to an inner anguish. Others rebel, perhaps being openly defiant, in an attempt to gain the attention that they have been long denied. Some drop out completely in order to avoid the pressure and find meaning elsewhere.

By fighting the authoritarian establishment, the rebel speaks for freedom and authenticity. Unconsciously, many students are supportive when a defiant student speaks out against a traditional teacher. They may be shocked that an individual student would take such a stance, recognizing that it can have devastating consequences and threaten the student's future in school. But some students report that, while they do not condone the inappropriate behavior toward a teacher, they were glad to see a particular teacher "put in her place" and to "feel some heat" from a putdown. Maslow's admonishment still applies:

> *...Let people realize clearly that every time they threaten someone or humiliate or hurt unnecessarily or dominate or reject another human being, they become forces for the creation of psychopathology, even if these be small forces. Let them recognize that every man who is kind, helpful, decent, psychologically democratic, affectionate, and warm, is a psychotherapeutic force even though a small one* (Maslow, 1954, p. 321).

When students feel secure, they are more apt to take risks. This implies that if students are to explore ideas and feelings in the classroom, there must be a friendly, warm, understanding, and non-threatening atmosphere where students are encouraged to be open. In this type of learning environment, students will want to cooperate. They have the feeling that mistakes are of minor consequence and that the really important thing to do is to participate. The atmosphere encourages students to try and there is no punishment or loss of self-esteem if they do not totally succeed in their attempts.

New facts or ideas that are discomforting to one's self are more easily perceived and assimilated when external threats are minimal. For example, when students who already feel deficient in reading are forced to read aloud, ridiculed for the effort, and given failing grades, it is no surprise that many of these students continue through school with no appreciable increase in reading ability. Fear is crippling to individuals as it causes them to be continually on the defense. On the other hand, in a supportive, understanding environment where self-evaluation is encouraged, and where external threats are at a minimum, individuals can work with more confidence and increase their reading ability.

When there are few threats to the self, experience can be perceived in differentiated fashion and new learning can take place. This is an extension of the preceding idea. When poor readers are called upon to recite in class and panic, the words on the pages become unintelligible symbols. Thus, the students don't have much chance to demonstrate their reading skills. If students are in an environment which fosters personal security, they are free to perceive the symbols on the page in a differentiated fashion, to recognize differing elements in similar words, to perceive partial meanings, and to put them together. In this case, they move forward in the process of learning.

A teacher who facilitates personal growth does not threaten and is not threatened by students. Threat by either party causes both to be on guard. In a positive and non-threatening classroom atmosphere, students won't have to worry about maintaining their psychological defenses and they can grow and change.

The absence of threat does not imply the absence of challenge. Personal growth is facilitated when challenges are present. But, students must be prepared to meet challenges and feel confident in facing them. School should be a positive experience, a place to grow, make mistakes, and to learn from these mistakes. If we are to foster personal growth, then we will want to create a nonpunitive atmosphere, a place where students feel that they can speak out and explore ideas without fear of reprisal. Rather than placing ourselves in a position of stamping out mistakes, we want to help bring students' thinking into the open and help them clarify their thoughts and feelings.

Learning is Self-initiated

When students choose to participate in the learning process, learning is enhanced. Students should learn to make decisions, choose directions, and discover their own learning resources. They should be encouraged to formulate their own problems, to decide their own course of action in resolving the problems, and to live with the consequences of their choices. When this happens because they have chosen to take an active part in the process significant learning is taking place.

The value of self-initiated learning is that it involves the whole person, feelings as well as intellect. Learning about ourselves and putting the new knowledge into practice in everyday living is gut-level learning and it is the most pervasive and lasting kind. It is energizing. People who can put themselves into creative situations will discover valuable things about themselves and others, as well as ways in which problems or situations might be approached.

Being stimulated to explore a subject may enhance learning, but the sense of discovery, of reaching out, and of grasping and comprehending must come from within the learner. Therefore, the most effective kind of learning is self-initiated.

Sometimes people will experience an immediate and physical need to learn about a subject and they will initiate the learning process. A diabetic, for instance, may be motivated to learn about medical procedures, diets, and so forth as a part of a need to enhance physical survival. At other times a person's psychological need to survive will be sufficient motivation to initiate learning. Whatever the cause, the desire to learn is a natural part of the organism.

Stop for a moment and think about yourself in terms of those things you can remember and do the easiest. Are these things that you sought out or were they things that were forced on you? For example, most of us enjoy listening to an inspiring speaker, but can you remember what was said the last time you heard one? Or, were you left with a general impression, perhaps a few selected words.

Do you remember what the speakers spoke about on your gradua-tion days? On the other hand, how much do you recall from what you presented in speeches, in contrast to what you heard others present?

Learning is Self-evaluated

Who should be held accountable for what is learned? Who ultimately decides the value of a learning experience? Certainly, teachers want to share in an evaluation process, but learning is a personal and individual matter that calls for self-evaluation.

A student's failure is of concern to teachers, friends, and society. But, what are the standards by which the failure is determined? Many times it is a case of one child being compared to others. A "standard norm" might be used to tell where a student should be at a particular time in growth, development, and achievement. Perhaps we should begin to think in terms of what a person has achieved rather than where that person has failed. Do you look at your successes or count your failures?

For some, success is being first in something. For years, our schools have taught this concept of success. Teachers use competi-tion both as a means of motivating students and as a means of iden-tifying those who they suspect will fail in subsequent tasks or be successful in later years. They are pleased to write the latter letters of recommendation.

Teacher preparation programs are replete with competitive games and techniques that are designed to stimulate learning in the classroom. The facilitative teacher, however, knows that it can be difficult to facilitate personal growth of all participants in an at-mosphere of competition.

Some people argue that learning to cope with such forces in life is one of the most valuable things a child can learn in school, especially since they are such a prominent part of life in the United States. Most parents like to brag about their children's achieve-ments and push them to excel. However, those students who find themselves in the fast-track of competition when they are unprepared for it may experience excessive stress. This is especially true when it threatens friendships. Too high of expecta-tions, intense competition, and social pressure can cause problems in forming relationships between peers, parents, and teachers. As one observer noted, "Competition tends to bring out the best in products and the worst in people."

The pressure of intense competition can lead to excessive anxiety, fear, and frustration. It can deter learning. Competition can also discourage some students from wanting to facilitate their classmates or friends in the learning process. For instance, some discourage others from being successful and secretly, if not openly, hope that others will fail, thus making them look better. Or, they might be jealous when others succeed and be unable to acknowledge their successes. In most of our schools someone's failure is used to reflect another's success.

When students try to defeat each other in competition for grades and for recognition, they're damned if they do and damned if they don't. When they lose, they can be hostile toward those who have beaten them. If they win, they can be the target of hostility from those who have lost. Competition can be motivating and spur people to perform their best, thus making friends proud and more supportive. Or it can be destructive to friendships and detrimental to overall personal growth. Facilitative teachers recognize both aspects and help students to identify and discuss their feelings before they say or do harmful things to one another.

Unfair competition could be a major cause of student dropouts. In classrooms where competition dominates, there is someone who continually loses. A person can cope with only so much failure and rejection. Thus, perhaps some students are not dropouts, but pushouts. Research indicates that the one of the most common causes of high school attrition is poor performance and lack of interest in school subjects. It is difficult to maintain interest in anything in which you continually fail.

There are other implications related to failure. Listen to this argument:

> *I don't think Johnny should be allowed to take my Spanish course; he only got a C in English. Everyone knows that if you can't do better than a C in English, you can't do well in Spanish.*

This teacher expects students to meet a predetermined standard before working with them. Yet, if relatively uneducated children or adults in Spain can learn to speak Spanish, it seems that most English speaking students in the United States could develop, with study and the help of a trained professional, a verbal facility in Spanish or some other foreign language. Or, is this a case of where the student must fit the system, rather than the system fit the student?

To employ a single set of criteria by which to judge the achievement of all students might be unfair, but it provides an easy
method of predicting academic success or failure. It can also give
people a predisposition regarding a child. That is to say, if a child
is placed in an ability level group, this too frequently becomes a
teacher's only guide as to the performance expected from that
child.

Ability does not always determine performance. If we do not look
beyond our measures of ability, we may as well decide very early
in a child's education whether or not that child will be successful.
When teachers openly behave toward students as though they are
competent or incompetent, chances are increased that those students will perform as predicted.

When self-criticism and self-evaluation are the basic components
of the learning process, and when evaluation by others is of secondary importance, independence, creativity, and self-reliance are
facilitated. Self-reliance blossoms in an atmosphere of self-evaluation. If children are to grow up to be independent and responsible,
they must be given opportunities at an early age to make their own
judgments and decisions and to evaluate the consequences of these
judgments and decisions.

Parents and teachers may provide information and models of
behavior, but it is the growing child who must evaluate one's own
behavior and come to conclusions as to what is best and appropriate. Children who are dependent both at school and at home on
the evaluations of others are likely to remain dependent, im-
mature, or explosively rebellious against all external evaluations
and judgments in later life. Learners must be involved in evaluating what it is that they are experiencing. They know whether it is
meeting their needs and whether or not it will lead toward what
they want to know. Ultimately, learners must decide if what is
being learned has any personal value.

Learning is Feeling-focused

In the teaching of any subject it is important that materials and
techniques have a feeling focus to them. Some educators have
referred to this as an affective base. That is to say, regardless of
subject matter or curriculum, the most fundamental psychological
basis for learning occurs when a student is emotionally involved.
Involvement means having an opportunity to identify and explore
feelings, especially as related to ideas and behaviors.

A school curriculum should be designed so that a student's feelings are a recognized part of the learning experience. This should not be taken to mean that subject content is less important. Knowledge of ideas is important. It gives us a personal resource that enables us to think about matters, to draw upon in everyday living. However, if personal growth is to occur, the intellectual aspects of the curriculum cannot be over emphasized at the expense of personal feelings.

Teaching styles that are directed to what students are feeling need not interfere with academic pursuits or goals. To the contrary, where teachers promote intellectual growth and emotional satisfaction, the result is more personal learning and higher student scores on achievement tests.

Students' feelings about themselves and their abilities play a large part in academic success. Studies of self-concept indicate that once one has a picture of oneself, it influences present and future performance. Therefore, any activity that enhances the student's self-concept improves academic performance and should be a high priority activity for teachers. Perhaps the best way to think of learning is that it is the process of thinking—feeling—doing. When these factors are maximized, learning is more effective, efficient, and purposeful.

Teachers are Learners Too

To facilitate personal growth in students, a teacher must first possess a high degree of self-awareness and a willingness to participate in the learning process. The following verse states the case well:

> *No printed word nor spoken plea*
> *Can teach young minds what men should be,*
> *Not all the books on all the shelves*
> *But what the teachers are themselves.*

> Anonymous

As teachers, we need to be aware of our own feelings, yearnings, impulses, and fantasies in order to provide the psychological openness that is a prerequisite to understanding the thoughts and feelings of others. We need to know how these feelings influence our behaviors and expectations from others. Students share and risk themselves only to the degree that we are willing to share ourselves and take similar risks.

As teachers, we are models of authenticity—or the lack of it. Self-awareness and acceptance of self and others is essential if we are to use the classroom to meet our needs and student needs in desirable ways.

Students will learn to recognize most of our feelings without our expressing them. We are important people in their lives. They tune-in to our feelings through our subtle cues, just as we do with them. Feelings are such an important part of the learning process that they should be brought into the open and viewed as a part of all learning and decision-making. If we are to facilitate personal growth, we must have the ability and the courage to enter into the lives of our students, feeling their failures, successes, triumphs, and disappointments. We must be willing to share their hurt and their pride.

As teachers, we want to facilitate personal growth in our students out of caring for others. We must be willing to disclose things about ourselves and permit other people to see us as we are, to know what we think, to know what we believe, to know what we cherish. If we expect students to grow, we must share our feelings as well as our thoughts. We must share in a way which does not demand or impose ourselves on others, but in a way which says that we too are growing and learning all the time.

As facilitators of learning, we need to recognize and accept our own limitations. There will be times when our behavior will not be very facilitative. At times it is difficult to keep an open mind, especially when student attitudes and ideas are markedly different from our own. We may even find ourselves becoming angry, suspicious, or intolerant. This is an important part of us, which if recognized, can be turned into a growth experience for us and the students.

Learning is facilitated through open communication in the classroom. Open communication means that our feelings and student feelings can be valued, shared, discussed, and related to intellectual concepts and plans. If we are caught at times between old and new approaches to learning, the most effective teaching will still take place when we communicate openly with our students. Through open communication we can learn what is important and meaningful to everyone. We'll learn how our work—or teaching—affects them and where the gaps exist. When communication is closed, we can only guess what kind of learning is taking place.

Some teachers are content to look at specific behavioral objectives and assume that these alone are enough to evaluate the effectiveness of learning. It is a mistake to think that a carefully defined curriculum, prescribing similar goals for all students and a precise plan for handling contingencies in the classroom, will automatically facilitate learning. The learning climate in a classroom is affected by all participants, all learners—including the teacher.

Chapter 2
The Facilitative Teacher

What Research Says About Teachers

What is a good teacher? The answer to this question is an illusive one. Millions of dollars and countless hours have been spent in order to define teaching and characterize an effective teacher. However, despite all these efforts, we are still seeking a better answer to the question: What is a good teacher? Let's take a closer look at a few of the most prominent issues.

The Teacher as a Scholar

Teachers need to know their subject. They need a knowledge base from which to structure learning experiences for students. They need not be someone who can answer all the questions posed by students. In that sense, a teacher has to be a scholar who can be an intellectual resource.

At first it was assumed that a person who had a vast storehouse of knowledge about a particular subject would make a good teacher. This belief was reflected in many of the early teacher education programs. It was not uncommon for the prospective teacher to hear lectures, take notes, and spend many hours wading through books and other published materials in order to know facts and store information. This emphasis upon effective teaching is coming into vogue again. It is being suggested in many educational circles that teacher preparation programs contain too many hours of methodology or pedagogy. And, that these hours need to be reduced in order to invest more time in classes that provide a knowledge base in the subject to be taught.

The American Association of School Administrators (1961) published a report, first commissioned in 1929, in which all the available research on good and poor teachers was reviewed. The research indicated that knowledge of subject matter or knowledge about good teaching methods did not insure superior performance by an individual teacher. Recent research still supports this conclusion (Guddemi, Swick, and Brown, 1987).

There is no argument here that methodology or pedagogy alone will suffice. It is, however, obvious to most of us that simply having an expert's knowledge about a subject is not enough to be a good teacher. How many times have you heard a college student say, "Bright person and really knows the field, but...." Interestingly enough, teachers and administrators often describe many of their best teachers without any reference to their knowledge or expertise. Certainly, it helps. But, most students learn information and facts best with the help of a facilitative teacher, one who is not only knowledgeable of the subject but also of interpersonal skills.

The Teacher as a Skilled Technician

If the mere possession of knowledge was not enough to define a good teacher, it was then assumed that an effective teacher was one skilled in teaching methods. In an early study, Barr (1929) was concerned with the characteristics of good and poor teachers. Using time charts, stenographic records, and many other observational techniques, he compiled a list of weaknesses of poor teachers. In descending order of weakness, the list included the following:

1. Inadequate provisions for individual differences
2. Overauthoritarian manner
3. Formal textbook teaching
4. Inability to stimulate pupil interest
5. Weak discipline
6. Inadequate daily preparation
7. Lack of interest in the work
8. Inadequate knowledge of subject matter

In this case Barr was really characterizing poor teaching, which is not too different from contemporary lists. Why teachers were poor and why they were perceived of as poor was not a part of his study. Consequently, little information was gained that would enable others to help teachers improve themselves. There followed a general trend in the recognition that teaching must be a part of one's personality. This concept is still considered relevant.

Sometimes teachers recognize that they are not doing an adequate job and that they need help. A study by Replogle (1950) identified several areas in which teachers wanted professional help:

1. Improving teaching methods and techniques
2. Utilizing principles of group dynamics
3. Locating community resources
4. Providing for individual differences
5. Handling pupil behavior and discipline cases
6. Meeting the needs of atypical students
7. Enabling teachers to evaluate their own teaching competence
8. Caring for the needs of the emotionally maladjusted
9. Relating the ongoing class activities to the problems, concerns, and tensions of the pupils
10. Using current teaching situations to make more understandable the contemporary social realities
11. Making better use of visual aids
12. Locating and making available expert resources and personnel, as special problems arise
13. Identifying the possibilities of the current classroom activity to enable pupils to better understand democratic values, loyalties, and beliefs
14. Constructing teaching units on problems and topics not found in basic textbooks.

An examination of this list clearly shows that many of the problems that were of concern to teachers were related to mental health and human relations. Yet, for a period of time there continued to be an emphasis on assisting teachers to learn new methods and techniques, games included, that would help them to motivate children in the classroom.

Morsh and Wildner (1954) reviewed the research efforts regarding teaching performance during the period 1900-1952. They concluded with the statement:

> No single, specific, observable teacher act has yet been found whose frequency or percent of occurrence is invariably and significantly correlated with student achievement. Yet, it appears that questions based on student interest and experience rather than assigned

subject matter, the extent to which the instructor challenges the students to support ideas and the amount of spontaneous student discussion, may be related to student gains.

This conclusion supports the idea that effective teaching is related to communication in the classroom. Because teaching is primarily a verbal process, many efforts have been made to analyze the verbal communication of student and teacher in the classroom. Since the Morsh and Wilder (1954) report, new information has been gained which suggests that some teacher behaviors are still more effective than others (Cruickshank, 1986; Gurney, 1987; Martin, 1988).

From numerous studies of classroom interaction, it has become clear that most teachers talk more than their students, from kindergarten to graduate school. There are many studies which draw attention to the impact that teacher talk has upon the learning process, but, for our purposes, only two important works will be discussed.

Neil Flanders (1970) was a pioneer in systematic observation in the classroom and he has summarized several studies based upon his systematic approach to analyzing classroom interaction. He found that teachers of high-achieving classes accepted, clarified, and used student ideas significantly more than teachers of low-achieving classes. Moreover, teachers in high-achieving classes criticized significantly less and encouraged significantly more student-initiated talk.

From his research Flanders developed the "rule of two thirds." This rule states that in the average classroom someone is talking two-thirds of the time; two thirds of the time the person talking is the teacher; and two-thirds of the time that the teacher talks, the teacher is using direct influence (lecture, direction-giving, criticism). However, the rule of two-thirds was modified for teachers of the high-achieving children and teachers of the low-achieving children.

The first part of the rule, that two-thirds of the time someone is talking, held for both groups, but the teachers of the low-achieving groups talked about 80 percent of the time while teachers of the high-achieving groups talked about 55 percent of the time. In the low-achieving groups, teachers used direct influence about 90 percent of the time, while teachers of the high-achieving groups used direct influence about 50 percent of the time.

Considering the fact that teacher effectiveness, in this study, was determined by both student attitude and achievement, one gets the impression that the indirect approach to teaching is much more effective than the direct approach, regardless of the grade level and the subject matter taught.

Another significant study on teaching was conducted by Amindon and Giammatteo (1967). They studied 153 elementary school teachers from 11 suburban districts in Pennsylvania. Using the Flander's system of interaction analysis, a profile of verbal patterns of superior teachers was prepared and compared to the profiles of a group of average teachers. The results of the study showed:

> Although the normative group and the superior group responded to feelings infrequently, the superior group used about three times as much acceptance of feeling responses than those in the normative group.
>
> Both groups used statements of praise and encouragement frequently, but the superior teachers used more praise after student-initiated ideas. They also gave reasons for praise more often than the normative group.
>
> The lecture, as a way of teaching, was used more by the average group of teachers in a continuous fashion. That is, the superior teachers were interrupted more frequently by questions during their lectures than the average teachers.
>
> The regular teachers gave twice as many directions as did the superior teachers.
>
> The average group of teachers used about twice as much criticism, particularly as a controlling technique for student noise.

It is obvious that teacher patterns in this study were different. Student patterns were also markedly different. Twice as many student-initiated statements occurred in classes taught by superior teachers. Whereas students participated about 40 percent of the time in the average class, in the classes of the superior teachers, students participated over 50 percent of the time.

The results indicated that superior teachers dominated their classrooms less, used indirect verbal behavior more and direction giving criticism less than the normative group of teachers. There was about 12 percent more student participation in the classes of superior teachers and student-initiated ideas were accepted more, encouraged more, and used to build upon for further discussion.

Surprisingly, this kind of interaction and the conclusions about teaching have persisted over the past few decades. In a recent analysis, the researchers concluded:

> Ironically, studies over time have persistently shown that if one is to learn to teach well, it is not enough to have a knowledge of subject matter, a knowledge of curricular materials and organization, a knowledge of educational psychology and child development, an understanding of social issues and a chance to practice teaching under the guidance of a supervised teacher. Nor will the picture change if we add liking children and having a strong desire to teach. What is essential, in addition, is for every teacher and prospective teacher to become engaged in the study of teaching and the acquisition of skill in the genuine "how" of teaching, that is, skill in the interactive talk which occurs during teaching activities. By analyzing, studying, and practicing behavior through the conscious selection and examination of verbal interaction during the various teaching activities, one can acquire teaching skill (Rogers, Waller, and Perrin, 1987).

It is important to note that a verbal response must be in one's repertoire of skills if one is to have the option of using it. It seems evident that too many teachers are working with a limited range of verbal skills. Certainly, this is one area that shows a great deal of promise in helping teachers to become more effective.

The Teacher as a Person

Because it has been difficult to identify "good" or "poor" methods of teaching, some educators have suggested that the teacher is an artist, one who is uniquely skillful in bringing about the desired results through a helping relationship. Good teachers find ways of using themselves, their talents, and their surroundings to assist their students to learn. Both effective and ineffective teachers recognize that the helping relationship is important in the classroom. Interesting enough, most teachers apparently know and can talk about the importance of being a helping person in the classroom, but not enough are able to put theory into practice.

Several attempts have been made to discover more about the teacher as a person and the teacher's impact upon the learning process. Researchers have compared the beliefs held by good and poor teachers about people in general. Studies indicate that good teachers possess an internal rather than external frame of reference. The good teacher is also more concerned with perceptual experiences rather than objective events. Moreover, good teachers perceive others as having the capacity to look at their own problems, to view others with dignity and as non-threatening and who are capable of enhancing their personal growth (Gurney,1987).

Research further indicates that good teachers are sensitive to others and see themselves as adequate, trustworthy, and able to help others. Finally, good teachers tend to see their purpose in teaching as one of freeing rather than controlling students. Good teachers tend to be personally involved in the learning situation and are concerned with the processes as much as achieving goals.

Almost three decades ago Emmerling (1961) discovered that high school teachers could be grouped according to the problems that they identified as the most urgent. One group was called the open or positively-oriented group. For these teachers their most serious learning problems occurred when they were unable to facilitate a child's learning. For example, they were concerned about helping children to think for themselves and to become independent, getting them to participate and to express special needs and interests. Whereas, the second group of teachers tended to see their problems in terms of student deficiencies and inabilities rather than potential.

For example, teachers in the positive group were concerned about teaching students who lacked a desire to learn, who were unable to listen or follow directions, and who lacked motivation. When students were asked to fill out a relationship inventory on all teachers, the positively oriented group of teachers were perceived as significantly more accepting, empathic, and genuine than the other group of teachers. It was concluded that the positively oriented teachers tried to facilitate learning. Others were less inclined to help students and depended upon their being willing and motivated to achieve.

The Teacher as a Facilitator of Personal Growth

Within the last decade we have learned a great deal about human behavior, about the teacher as a helper, and about helping relationships. Much of what we now know has come through careful analysis of helping relationships found in counseling and psychotherapy. To be successful as a counselor or therapist takes more than being an expert in the field of psychology; it is more than providing information and helpful insights; and, it is more than being thoroughly trained in counseling theory and procedures.

There was a time when we thought that lack of progress in therapy was probably because of some deep-seated problem that a client was unable to discuss. Or, if a client didn't function any better as a result of therapy, it was certainly a loss and a disappointment, but the patient probably was no worse off than before. It now appears that these naive assumptions can no longer be accepted. That is, we now know that therapy and counseling can be for better or for worse. In some cases clients actually deteriorate into a routine that is detrimental to their overall personal growth and development. The idea is frightening, but persons actually can be harmed in situations that were theoretically designed to enhance their growth.

Closer examination suggests that therapists can differ in approach, theoretical rationale, training, sex, personal values, and experience, but there seem to be some essential conditions in all successful counseling and therapy. When clients experience these conditions, they tend to become more fully functioning individuals. In general, these are: understanding, nonpossessive warmth, genuineness, respect, regard, caring, and acceptance (Brammer, 1988).

One gets the impression that an individual must experience a relationship that reduces defensiveness and opens the avenues for communication in a warm, close, non-threatening setting. Generally speaking, clients who show the most therapeutic change, as measured by various indices, perceive more of the helping conditions in their relationship with the counselor/therapist than those who show less change.

These same conditions are a part of classroom experiences. Teaching can be for better or for worse. We can no longer assume that if a student does not benefit from a teacher there will be a negligible effect. In reality, it is possible that some students can actually suffer when the helping conditions are not present.

We believe that high-facilitative teachers are those who reflect or create the essential helping characteristics. These highly functioning individuals have a positive effect on students. A truly child-centered or person-centered approach to teaching nourishes these conditions. They are at the center of facilitative teaching and teacher success.

How can teachers create these conditions? What do they need to do with students? What things must be considered when developing a lesson plan, leading a class discussion, or resolving a classroom problem?

This book attempts to address these issues. But first, let's look at what some students say about teachers.

What Students Say About Teachers

The authors have talked with many students about their school experiences. Two themes predominate when children give negative reports about school. The first usually deals with frightening or embarrassing experiences, resulting from the actions of unkind or insensitive teachers and classmates. Students have told about incidents of harsh punishment, acts of sarcasm and ridicule, and times when they felt a loss of personal dignity. The second theme usually centers on feelings of boredom which stemmed from meaningless tasks and lack of personal involvement.

Strangely enough not too much is known about how young children themselves look upon their school experience. This fact is particularly surprising in a day when it has become almost a national past-time to find out how people feel about things. We seem to be mildly interested in student opinion by the time students have reached high school and college campuses. But, it is more common than not to dismiss student opinion or not to ask at all.

Magazines and newspapers sometimes feature true-life stories written by dropouts, who tell about their dislike for school. When one listens carefully to their experiences and explores their complaints, it is easy to conclude that many were pushed out and that school was so unpleasant that it negatively shaped their lives.

The nation's schools fail to reach approximately 25 percent of the students who are required to attend. When a student decides to drop out of school, that student is saying in a loud, clear voice that school has no special meaning, that no one cares, that school personnel are not interested or helpful, and that there are better places to be in order to gain a sense of worth and value.

We have some idea of what research has revealed about good and poor teachers, but what about the students who successfully completed many years of formal education? Perhaps the students who have succeeded in school can tell us about the kinds of teachers who were the most helpful to them.

Over the past several years one of the authors has been collecting a series of papers from undergraduate and graduate students regarding their experiences with both poor and good teachers. Over 400 students wrote papers which described teachers who had a significant influence on them and their education. They were asked to describe two teachers—one who "had positive impact, someone who they still value" and another one who "had a negative impact, someone with whom they would not like to spend any more time."

The following are excerpts selected from these papers:

No. 1—Female (positive)

> *Mr. Jessup was a very warm and understanding person. He was friends with all of his students and was active in student activities. As a teacher he was fair and honest with his students which made studying a lot more fun. In class he always included his students in every lecture. He never stood in front of the class and lectured without getting all or most of the students involved. He would bring in different ideas—he was someone that each student could trust and feel important around, because he took an interest in our problems. He was willing to listen and help solve anything that might be disturbing to us no matter how small it seemed... in sum, he genuinely cared.*

(Negative)

> *She never had a smile and she always addressed her students with a formal Miss or Mr. The atmosphere in her room was a feeling of tension and hostility. She punished students harshly. If a student gave a wrong answer, she made it a point to humiliate that student. This made me feel insecure and I felt totally lost in her class. I would never answer or ask questions because it would be too embarrassing. She had a great deal to do with my disliking math in any form. I used to enjoy math and always received good grades until her class.*

This student felt threatened by the punitive approach used by this last teacher and it was crippling to the point that "I would never answer or ask questions...." The sad result was "I used to enjoy math...." Humiliation is not an effective motivator.

No. 2—Male (Negative)

> *She showed obvious partiality to her favorite students. They were the ones who always got the special tasks and they were the only students with whom she would speak civilly to. The rest of us felt like scum under her feet. Her chief method for making us work harder and perform better was ridicule. It wasn't a fun and games atmosphere, but one in which feelings were hurt and egos were trampled upon.... I believe I disliked her most because she was insensitive to junior high school kids. She was cold and sarcastic.... She never seemed to take our feelings into consideration.*

(Positive)

Mrs. Raverez was involved with each of her students. She not only worked with the more popular ones, but made every individual a special concern to her. Her door was always open and we could talk to her about anything. She was involved in many activities outside of her classroom and this made her closer to the students. Her biggest asset was communication. She gave suggestions and helpful hints, but never forced us to do things her way. I still visit with her when I am home from college.

This young man was turned off by the one teacher who had favorites and was turned on to the one who treated all her students with special concern. He still visits with that positive teacher when he returns home. What happens to those tough-minded teachers that some principals hold in high esteem and tell their students, "One day you'll be glad he was rough on you and you'll come back to thank him."

No. 3—Female (Negative)

How easy it is to remember those teachers you wish would vanish from your mind, those teachers who embarrassed you, scolded you, and tried to mold you into something you didn't want to be.

I can remember a time when Mrs. Swanson, my French teacher, kept me repeating a word over and over because I could not say it correctly. Over and over again, I mispronounced it. Finally, after a ten-minute session in front of the class, she gave up. Suddenly I started to cry, I was so emotionally upset that she turned on me and said, "Look at that little cry baby." I felt so embarrassed and ashamed. This is a vivid memory in my mind and I will probably never forget it.

I can't deny that Mrs. Swanson was knowledgeable, yet her teaching methods were very poor. She felt that ridiculing and embarrassing students were the best ways to help them learn. Most of her students, including me, lived in deadly fear of her. We held our breath when we entered her classroom and exhaled after the 45-minute session. The best feeling of the day was leaving her class and knowing that we had survived one more time.

(Positive)

In contrast, the best teacher I had was one I could trust and who I thought of as my friend. My sixth grade teacher Mrs. Madigan, believed in me. Until that time I don't remember any other teachers paying particular attention to me. I was a shy, skinny girl who lacked confidence. Being the youngest in my family, I learned to listen more than talk. I don't know what it is that she did, but somehow she instilled in me a feeling of belief about myself. She believed in me and I came to believe in myself. I think that children can sense this feeling in a teacher....

This student indicated that she was shy and constantly threatened in the first teacher's room, "the best feeling of the day was leaving her classroom...." The tremendous threat gave her tunnel vision. All she could think about was self-survival. In contrast, the most effective teacher was one that recognized her shyness and lack of confidence and instilled a feeling of self-worth.

No. 4—Male (Positive)

Mrs. Arnesen was my fifth grade teacher. She immediately comes to mind when I think about who was my best teacher. She was in love with people and in love with life. She always had a smile on her face. I remember how I used to feel sorry for her when she had to discipline a student because I think that was the hardest part of teaching for her.... Mrs. Arnesen is about the only teacher I ever had that I thought of more as a person than a teacher. What I mean by this is that most teachers hid themselves behind their desks. Mrs. Arnesen was a teacher and a person at the same time. She was never afraid of being herself.

.....She knew her students as people. I believe she knew me better than any teacher I ever had. Her being so personal was very important to me. Since I was going through adolescence, it was very helpful to have a teacher who thought of me not as a student, but as a person. Mrs. Arnesen was by far the best teacher I ever had. She was the best because she was so full of love.

(Negative)

The worst teacher comes to mind because it was a frustrating experience for me. It was a university education course, of all things! The teacher was boring. The teacher could not communicate. Nobody could figure out what he expected of us. The interesting part was that he was supposed to be teaching us how to teach and, yet, he was the worst teacher most of us had ever experienced. I have never really been able to understand why he was so poor.

He seemed interested in being a good teacher. One time we took two class periods to talk with him about the class and its procedures. It didn't accomplish much because the only things that we could tell him was that the class was boring and that it dragged. I think his problem was that he was too impersonal. He knew all the latest educational research but used it to manage us as a bunch of sheep instead of working closely with us.

How often have you heard the comment from a teacher, "My students don't see me as a person with a family, friends, and so forth." Why? The student above indicated that one teacher shared himself, he was "more of a person than a teacher...." The two go together.

No. 5—Male (Negative)

The fear of authority was instilled in me in the third grade.... By remaining extremely quiet and obedient, I escaped most of her wrath with the exception of one subject, math. I was a very poor math student and I had trouble identifying numbers and number concepts. Mrs. Baker valued oral recitation in math and she would tell us to "quickly" turn to page so and so in our math books and then she would immediately begin calling on students to answer questions 1, 2, and so forth. I could never find the right page quick enough and she would usually call on me first.

As a result I would become terrified and panicked which resulted in another five-minute delay while I frantically looked for the right page. I remember the numbers blurring and my mind becoming a total blank so that when I finally did find the right page I couldn't answer the question. She would usually give me an exasperated look and call on someone else. I used to become physically sick in her class. I felt trapped and closed in. I rarely raised my eyes from the top of my desk. The year was a loss as far as educational progress went. I spend the entire third grade enduring this agony and it was harmful to the degree that even today I become anxious and fearful when I have to take a math course.

(Positive)

> *...He seemed to care about his students and he seemed to care about making the courses interesting to us. He was friendly, warm and concerned. He did not make fun of our questions or give smart intellectual type answers. He treated each person with respect and consideration. He "rapped" with us and he was on our side all the way. The class was happy, alive, and exciting. The students interacted with each other and the class got to be almost like a family. I'm not idealizing, it was really that great. I finally went to him with a personal problem because I had reached a deadend and I discovered that his concern for students was genuine. He listened to me and he gave me solid advice. This man helped me through a very difficult situation and he instilled in me a renewed interest in learning.*

Can you remember your teachers saying, "Quickly now, turn to page 20," and then asking you a question before you got to the page? Evidently this happened frequently to this student. Do you remember those teachers in your life who had a knack for calling on you when you didn't have the answer?

No. 6—Male (Negative)

> *...I rather fancy Mr. Zimmerman must have always had frustrated desires to be king, for in class he was king. The class was made up of peasants, all lucky to be there.*
>
> *On the first day of class, Mr. Zimmerman strode up and down in front of the room and announced his laws—no yawning, no coughing, no sneezing, no talking, etc., etc. Infractions of any rules resulted in a lowered conduct grade. Having no real control over my biological functions (I frequently yawned), it is needless to say that I had a string of F's in conduct. Mr. Zimmerman sent me out of the room frequently the first few days for having a cold. He possibly was a king with a germ phobia. Anyhow, how could his kingdom survive without him for a day? Not being able to ask questions, I fell quickly behind. But I must say one thing improved. By the third week I no longer got sent out of class.... I learned the fine art of skipping.*

Teachers can be king—king of the castle (classroom)—and can dispense success or failure at whim. The "king" described above probably had very long days because of his unruly peasants. Contrast this with the following teacher whom the student thought to be most positive.

(Positive)

> *...Relaxed, informal class discussion was encouraged and this included the expression of personal opinion and the discussion of individual work. The teacher was a good listener and was available for help outside of class. (In all fairness I should say that teacher No. 1 was also probably available for such help, but it would never have occurred to me to approach him. He was above me.)*

No. 7—Male (Negative)

> *Thinking about teachers who turned me off, one stands out in particular. It has been 14 years since I sat in Mrs. Schmidt's third grade room, but the memories of her are still very vivid. I've learned that when someone is under a great deal of emotional stress, the memory burns deeply. I was very scared of Mrs. Schmidt and I remember many bad times that I had with her.*

> *She was a tall woman and she used corporal punishment to maintain a silent classroom. I loved to move around and one day she actually tied me to the seat and left me there all day. I wet my pants and she ridiculed me for it. After that it was pure hell. I had to sit near her desk and I got into the habit of chewing a handkerchief and pulling off my shoes. My mouth was taped several times. My shoestrings were often the same strings that were used to tie me to my desk.*

> *I fell behind in everything except reading and my work was messy. She tried to remedy the underachievement by force rather than understanding and encouragement. I begged for a transfer, as did several other children, but my parents forced me to remain "under her rule" because teachers were supposed to know "what is best for students."*

> *...It took a long time for me to overcome my fear of teachers in general because of Mrs. X. I particularly remember her harsh treatment of another boy who turned out to be retarded. She instilled in me a dislike of school and a distrust of teachers that has undoubtedly affected my school achievement. I wonder how many others she has turned off to the value of learning?*

This young man spent about 1,000 hours, while in the third grade, under the tutelage of an insensitive and unkind individual. Her method of maintaining silence was by force and humiliation; and, 14 years later, "the memory burns deeply."Contrast this with the teacher described below, one that he had 4 years later in the seventh grade.

(Positive)

> *My seventh grade teacher made knowledge come alive for us, because knowledge was alive for him. He valued the uniqueness of each student. He made history and geography dynamic, real, and challenging. He used a variety of books and resources and encouraged us to pursue our individual interests. He had a wonderful sense of humor which brought fun into the classroom and into our lives. He inspired us to keep going even when the path was rough.... I admired his openness and his willingness to let us be ourselves.*

Student no. 7 and the previous six used basically similar terms and words to describe both their negative and positive experiences with past teachers. Even though the teachers described range from lower elementary grades to the college level, those terms used to describe the most ineffective or negative teachers were typically:

insensitive	arbitrary
cold	sarcastic
disinterested	demanding
authoritarian	punitive
ridiculing	disciplinarian

Interestingly, those teachers characterized as positive teachers were consistently described as having the qualities of:

good listeners	knowledgeable
empathic	trusting
caring	friendly
concerning	sense of humor
genuine	dynamic
warm	able to communicate
interested	

The following appeared in a Florida newspaper. The well-known local editor takes us back to when he was in the third grade.

MAKE KINDLING OF THOSE
SCHOOL HICKORY STICKS*

Readin' and ritin and rithmatic, taught to the tune of a hickory stick.

A 13-year-old... sixth-grader was paddled for using profanity. After the third swat he cried "enough." And then he turned around and punched the principal. Add to the boy's baggage a criminal battery conviction.

Our state is a hickory stick state. Our policy-makers approve of the occasional application of work to the unruly bottom. It's good for the kids. It teaches them discipline. It makes them behave.

And, of course, it leaves no lasting bruises. But my sympathies are with the boy. I call what he did self-defense. I call what the principal did to him child abuse.

Child abuse is what happened to me more than three decades ago—only I wasn't big enough to defend myself. And never mind that nonsense about no lasting bruises—I carry with me to this day the imprint of that abuse.

Let me tell you about child abuse in the third grade, as it was practiced in ... Pennsylvania, during the 1950s.

But first, I must make a confession. I can't write. I'm a professional journalist and I can't write. Oh, I can process words. The keyboard is my salvation. But I can't write.

I'm ashamed of my handwriting. Bank tellers and store clerks do a double take when I sign a check or a credit card receipt. Sometimes, when asked to initial a stack of expense requests at the office, I wonder if some eagle-eyed auditor will notice that the unsightly scrawl on the last voucher resembles not at all the unsightly scrawl on the first.

I type personal notes and letters, or I handprint them. That's because I have the handwriting of a child. It's always been a sore point with me. But I've always blamed myself. I assumed that I was a lazy student back when we were all learning the basics. I got the readin' part all right; and I even got by in the rithmatic' department. But somehow, ritin' never caught on.

But then, a few years ago, a chance conversation with an aunt of mine put my childish handwriting in a new light.

It turns out that I'm a right-handed writer trapped in a left-handed body. I've never thought much about being left-handed. It sort of slips through in a dozen sub-conscious ways. I eat with my left hand. Sometimes, when I reach my office door in the morning—a stack of newspapers clutched in my left arm—I find myself, in annoyance, reaching around with my right hand to dig my keys out of my left side pocket—because that's where I had casually slipped them upon getting out of my van a few minutes earlier.

Still, I've always considered myself right-handed. That's because I write, after a fashion, with my right hand. At least, I have since the third grade. Let me tell you about Mrs. Marley.

If pressed, I don't think I could name more than one or two of my teachers in the fourth, fifth, sixth, or seventh grades. But I've never forgotten my third-grade teacher. And, until that chance conversation with my aunt, I've never really known why.

Mrs. Marley has always been there in the back of my mind. Her stern visage. Her gray hair. Her no-nonsense manner. Her ruler. Most of all I remember her ruler. I remember it moving up and down, from desk to desk. I remember the sound of it. Its crack on little hands and fingers... the answering yelp of pain, or startled cry.

Mrs. Marley was an "old fashioned" teacher, or so my aunt told me a few years ago. She didn't believe that children should be "encouraged" to indulge in aberrant behavior—like left-handed writing. She knew how to correct that sort of nonsense.

Mrs. Marley trained only right-handed writers.

Mrs. Marley and her ruler.

Soon, I will be 40, and Mrs. Marley has been with me all these years. I wonder how surprised she would be to know that my handwriting has improved hardly at all since I left her classroom—since I learned it to the tune of her hickory stick.

I wonder if she would be pleased to know that she has had more lasting influence on me than any other teacher.

I wonder how many other children—now parents them-selves—had similarly bad habits drummed out of them by Mrs. Marley and her ruler. I wonder how many of them would wish for their children to learn their lessons the "old fashioned" way.

I know, teachers don't do that sort of thing anymore. Left-ies are allowed to be lefties. Corporal punishment is now a formal procedure—executed in the the principal's office, not administered pell mell in the classroom.

But things haven't really changed all that much. Two years ago, when an elementary school principal in Belle Glade wanted to beat the bad habit of speaking Creole in-stead of English out of an 11-year-old Haitian girl, he so impressed her that he fractured her arm. But, of course, it was her fault—the child had foolishly tried to defend her-self by raising her arm against the descending paddle.

So I call corporal punishment what it is, child abuse. And I hope that by the time my infant daughter reaches school age, Florida will have broken all of its hickory sticks. I do not like to imagine the terrible scene that might ensue be-tween Jenny's father and the petty, stick-wielding tyrant who seeks to beat the aberrant behavior out of her.

*Reprinted with permission from R. Cunningham, Gainesville Sun, Gainesville, Florida (January 23, 1988).

Although Mr. Cunningham says that he "can't write," he, like the others cited in this chapter, are considered among the most suc-cessful graduates. They made it through academic programs in high school, were admitted to and graduated from reputable universities. They described their positive teachers in terms of having or being able to create basic facilitative conditions—respect, warmth, and understanding along with having com-munication skills. When these conditions were not present, the same students experienced and remembered a negative experience in school. How many negative experiences does it take to make a failure? Which negative and positive experiences do you remem-ber?

Characteristics of a Facilitative Teacher

There are probably many teachers who have one or more of the characteristics which describe a facilitative teacher. "Now there is a good teacher," people might say. Some people describe effective teachers as "outstanding" and "wonderful." Yet, they may not be certain as to what makes the teacher so successful. In similar fashion, parents clamor to have their children placed in the "best" teachers' classrooms, while administrators, knowing that they play an important part in creating a school's image and reputation, wish that all teachers had such success.

What do they do? What are they like? What can we learn from them?

Some selected characteristics frequently identify teachers who are high facilitators of personal growth and achievement and who are recognized as most effective by students, parents, administrators, and their colleagues. In general, facilitative teachers are:

1. Attentive
2. Genuine
3. Understanding
4. Respectful
5. Knowledgeable
6. Communicative.

Let's look at each of these characteristics in more detail.

The Facilitative Teacher is Attentive

Problems in communication often result from inattentiveness and poor listening. Although it seems like a simple thing to do, and we often take it for granted, being attentive is an effort that requires skill. Being attended to and having an opportunity to talk about a matter is a pleasurable experience. For instance, when you feel that someone has *really* taken time to listen to you and that what you say has been received with understanding, you probably feel important. In addition, there is usually a sense that you feel closer to the person who has been listening to you.

Unfortunately, the vast majority of people are not effective listeners. You may not encounter very many during your lifetime. Sometimes, people seek out counselors and therapists because they know that they will have a chance to talk and be heard. How often do you think people in your life listen to your words and feelings? How do you know if they have really heard you?

The next time that you are with a group of people, note how well each attends and responds to you and the others. Unless it is an unusual group, the conversation will jump quickly from one person to another, with little (i.e. two-way) communication.

One person might start by expressing a concern about the control and discipline of students in the school. The usual response from someone who is "listening" is to relate that particular idea to their own experience, without responding directly to the speaker. For example, "You know *I've* been thinking of the same thing. ...And, I've decided...." At this point the focus moves to a new talker, leaving the original talker to wait another turn.

As we examine everyday listening experiences and habits, and perhaps take note of our own behaviors, we recognize that many times a listener is simply waiting for a speaker to stop talking so that person can say something. Subsequently, many listeners hear only the first few words spoken, and then their minds rush rapidly ahead to their own concerns and reactions. In most cases, the periods of silence while listeners are waiting a turn to speak, represents a period of tolerance more than a period of attentive listening.

Picture yourself in a group. How many times have you sat there tuning in and out of the discussion? What do you do as the conversation drifts from person to person? It may seem as if a collection of unrelated sounds and visual impressions are dominating the group.

Listening is affected by motivations and feelings. These change, of course, even as the conversation moves along which makes listening a shifting process. Attentive listeners know how to stay focused on the talker and to absorb what is being said before jumping to conclusions or offering a quick reaction.

Attentive listeners want to know more about others. They want to know what another person is thinking and feeling. Subsequently, they have a powerful influence on the way in which relationships, as well as the flow of the conversations, are formed. When we are unable to focus our attention on someone, we may be reacting to some hidden feelings or motives. This preoccupation with our own interests and thoughts can communicate that we do not care what is being said and the person talking might feel rejected or dismissed as unimportant.

Our attentiveness tends to be selective. From everything that a person is saying, we listen for that which is most pertinent to us. All of us learn to be selective listeners because there is a desire to both enhance ourselves and to find some way in which we can identify with the speaker. We seldom tolerate ambiguity or incongruence when someone is trying to explain something. Many people have the habit of interrupting or rushing in to correct matters.

We can all be more attentive listeners. For example, we might be sitting in a restaurant and trying to enjoy dinner and conversation with friends. An objective analysis of sounds in the room might show a clutter of noise—sounds from the kitchen, scuffling feet, clanging glasses, and other people talking around us. Yet, if we are really interested in what a friend is saying, we will give close attention and hear that person. We will be able to shut out the other things around us, unless someone brings into our awareness a particular distracting sound. Of course, if our attention wanes, then we will be suddenly aware of the distractions.

Attending might be described as the process of acknowledging particular stimuli from an environment. Thus, listening is a selective process in which we choose from the things around us that most fit our needs, purposes, and desires. Sometimes we select a stimulus because of its suddenness, intensity, or contrast to what we have been experiencing. At other times there might be sounds—stimuli—that we hear automatically because of habit. We focus upon things to which we have learned to attend.

If a listener expects to hear some expressed anger, there is a higher probability that the speaker will be perceived as being angry. The effects of such "mind sets" are significant. They can be detrimental to effective listening, especially if the listener jumps to conclusions and is unwilling to hear the person tell all of the story. Unfortunately, we are not always aware of our mind sets and they are at times difficult to control. Listening habits that help us go beyond what we expect in a situation can be valuable.

Attentive and careful listening also involves hearing "deeper levels" of communication. Good listeners not only attend literally to words, but they also make a special effort to understand the personal meanings of the speaker's words. In this case the listeners tune in on the feelings and attitudes that are underneath the content of the words. The listener who wants to be a facilitator hears the words and the feelings that add special meaning.

Guidelines for Effective Listening. The importance of being a good listener is a popular topic and many guidelines have been described. Among the most appropriate are:

1. Look directly at the person who is speaking. Good eye contact suggests that you are attending to what is being said.

2. Avoid being preoccupied with your own thoughts. Don't rush ahead with your own ideas; rather, give attention to the way things are being said, the tone of the voice, the particular words or expressions being used, and bodily gestures.

3. Listen for feelings. A speaker's feelings are an important part of communication.

4. Say something to the speaker that will show that you are listening carefully, which encourages the speaker to talk more about the subject.

5. Behave in a non-evaluative way, being sensitive and aware of the speaker as a person.

The Facilitative Teacher is Genuine

Effective listening and understanding inevitably depend upon a person's genuine interest. Are you genuinely concerned about how one thinks and feels? Do you genuinely care to know?

"Tell it like it is" is still a popular expression. Students are especially suspicious of adults who talk one way and live another. Young people deplore hypocrisy. They want people to be trustful, honest, and genuine with them. Genuineness implies authenticity. You cannot be genuine if you are playing a role. Rather, genuineness denotes being in tune with your self and acting in a way that reveals congruence. It is extremely difficult to feel one thing and communicate another, as the truth will win out.

Genuineness could be the most important characteristic in a helping relationship. It sometimes makes "helpers" out of persons in your school simply because students can depend on them for honest responses. On the other hand, some persons, even though they have studied under the best instructors and know many techniques, still play at being a helper, a teacher, or a facilitator. If you play a role that is not characteristic of yourself, then your ability to facilitate others may be limited.

Students will know if we are playing at being genuine. Being genuine with a student implies direct personal encounter. This is an open meeting of minds, on a person-to-person basis without defensiveness. There is no attempt to retreat to a facade or a role. Genuineness is being open and aware of one's own experiences.

There is no real alternative to genuineness in a teaching relationship. even if we are shrewd and very skilled, it is still doubtful if we could hide real feelings from students. When we pretend to care, pretend to respect, or pretend to be open to experiences, we fool only ourselves.

The Facilitative Teacher is Understanding

Being genuine is important. However, it does not mean necessarily that a person will understand another. As we discover a student's perceptions, we begin to understand that student. Being genuine and listening attentively helps us to be empathic.

Empathy means fully understanding another person, at both cognitive and emotional levels. It involves going beyond the mere expression of words and intellectual ideas to a deeper level of communication. Empathy means coming to know, to value, and to respect another person from that person's frame of reference.

You have probably heard the expression, "Put yourself in the other person's shoes." This does not mean you must try to be that other person. Rather, when you have empathic understanding with a student, you have an awareness of that student's internal frame of reference. However, you don't need to lose your own frame of reference. It means that for a few moments you are united with the student. You're reading that person. You're feeling that you know what the student is experiencing. You sense that person also knows you are being understanding, although you probably will never comprehend or know everything that the student is experiencing.

Your attempts to perceive and respond to feelings, more than anything else, tells students that you are trying to understand. Moreover, they respect and appreciate these attempts even when you are not always accurate. The more accurate the empathy, the more credit you get. Being empathic puts a "chip in the bank" towards the development of a non-threatening, facilitative relationship. A few "chips in the bank" statements can help create the teacher/student bond that is needed for effective learning.

Students come to know themselves and their feelings better through empathic understanding. Letting them know that we are trying to understand also provides opportunities for self-initiated change. There is, unfortunately, considerable evidence that empathic understanding is not a characteristic of the general population. However, it is an interpersonal skill which can be learned. "Tuning-in" to students is a skill that can be acquired, but it takes practice.

The Facilitative Teacher is Respectful

Respect for individuals means recognizing and accepting their experiences as important influences on their lives. All people have the human potential for joy, depression, success, and failure. It is not easy to be perfect and few accomplish such a lofty goal. In addition, it is an illusive goal that is not easy to define. Yet, we often judge people by some mysterious set of standards that reflect a desire for perfection.

True respect indicates a concern for the student as a special person with unique feelings and experiences. This encourages us to search for the real person rather than rushing in to approve or disapprove.

Respect does not mean agreement. To respect another person as a human being implies that we value that person's feelings and worth. It does not mean that we must agree with their actions or approve of their behaviors.

Respect goes beyond optimism or simple reassurance. It is the communication of deep interest and concern. A high positive regard for students emphasizes that their dignity is valued, their feelings are accepted, and that they are not being judged as good or bad. The degree to which a teacher communicates respect for students helps define teacher-student relationships. If we feel and show positive regard for students, then they feel more positive toward us and are more willing to explore ideas and behaviors with us. Mutual respect opens the doors to learning.

Some students have low self-respect and their learning is impaired. They don't have much personal regard for themselves. In most cases it is because their feelings and behaviors were not accepted or valued. They may have felt put-down or rejected. As these students begin to experience respect, they may stop "defending" themselves long enough to examine new patterns of living and thinking. A teacher's positive regard, warmth, and respect can be communicated, breaking down barriers of isolation and paving the way for self-esteem.

The Facilitative Teacher is Knowledgeable

So far we have given primary attention to what some call the affective domain of teaching. However, facilitative teachers are also concerned with knowledge. They are thoroughly familiar with their subject matter.

Outstanding teachers have a love of knowledge and a desire to help their students discover the personal meanings that knowledge can have for them. Knowledge of subject matter is an essential part of being a good teacher. A teacher who is knowledgeable is a resource, someone who can make timely suggestions and offer valuable insights. Facilitative teachers want to help students to become more knowledgeable through their own experiences and serve as a catalyst in the learning process.

For instance, surveys of teachers in the United States suggest that most of them represent white-middle class America. Several books have been published which describe how teachers have suffered when they were forced to work in a situation that calls for knowledge of the culturally different. That is, in addition to knowledge of the subject matter and knowledge of communication skills, there is a need for teachers to know the general background and environmental situations of their students.

In some cases, you will have a classroom of students who represent several cultural or religious beliefs. It would be foolhardy to ignore these differences and assume that all students approach the same topic with the same values and attitudes. In addition, to ignore student backgrounds and experiences is to ignore valuable resources and opportunities for learning. Students learn from each other, especially in the presence of a facilitative teacher who knows the subject and appreciates positive differences.

The Facilitative Teacher is Communicative

Much of what society is and much of what it will become is an outcome of communication skills. People are a vital part of our lives. We need others in order to be fulfilled as persons and to experience our human potentiality. In fact, much of what we are as individuals and what we will become is a result of our relationships and ability to communicate with other people.

When our interpersonal relationships are positive and open, we can experience all our humanness and move toward personal fulfillment. We can learn and help others to learn. We feel alive and enjoy life. On the other hand, when our relationships lack personal involvement or when they restrict our personal growth, than we feel depersonalized and this can be reflected in a joyless kind of existence.

Facilitative teachers know the value of effective interpersonal skills. Communication in the classroom is dependent upon them. These teachers also know that effective interpersonal skills do not just happen by chance. They are learned. They take practice. They need to be used until they are a natural or integral part of our personal and working relationships.

Some people, albeit very few, were raised in families or special environments where effective interpersonal communication skills were a common part of their relationships with others. That is, adults in their lives demonstrated effective interpersonal skills for them every day. It was part of their day-to-day life. Therefore, the skills were easier to acquire as part of a natural consequence. Because their parents or significant others in their lives responded to them in facilitative ways, they learned—through modeling and direct experience—valuable communication skills.

Yet, even these people can benefit from carefully examining the evidence that has accumulated about working relationships and communication. Teaching requires a combination of interpersonal skills and communication patterns. It is a science. It is also an art, or seemingly natural talent, involving meaningful communication and the building of positive interpersonal relationships.

Facilitative teachers are sensitive to the impact of words on individuals. They are interested in a language of feelings as well as ideas. They know that although nonverbal communication plays an important part in relationships, verbal communication is a critical factor in the learning process. They know that words reflect attitudes and feelings. A few carefully chosen words can communicate an invitation to talk, to risk, to come closer. Ill chosen words push people away, close communication, threaten relationships, and impede learning.

Have you ever been in a situation where you were with someone, listening intently to what was being said, and suddenly feeling that you really understood what the person was saying and feeling? Then, just as suddenly, you were wondering and thinking, "What can I say now? I'm at a loss for words." Perhaps no words were necessary. Perhaps your being an attentive listener and being with the other person were helpful enough. Perhaps your genuine interest and respect were somehow communicated through gestures, eyes, or other nonverbal postures. But then again, perhaps some helpful word could have been said that communicated your caring, respect, and understanding.

Facilitative teachers recognize that communication between people is a skill, especially if one really cares. They know how to use facilitative responses and realize that not everyone has had training in interpersonal skills. Therefore, they are not afraid to assume more responsibility and take the lead in building relationships through facilitative responding.

Knowing the Culturally Different. A large percent of America's total population lives in cities of 50,000 or more today, or in areas which lead into these large cities. This concentration greatly intensifies social and economic problems that could conceivably destroy the structure of society. In addition, intercultural conflicts, which are discouragingly high, could increase.

How will America's schools cope with these problems? Educators hold the key to the process of reducing or eliminating the social and emotional barriers that prevent many ethnic minority group members from becoming productive citizens. The facilitative teacher makes concerted efforts to know the different cultural groups in the school and their influence on the learning environment.

A basic reason for the lack of such understanding of other cultures is the prescriptions about American behavior, standards of conduct, and morality were determined by middle and upper-class college graduates. It is evident that the ordinary middle-class white is caught up in the notion of assumed similarity. That is, they often feel that everyone is like them, or should be; therefore, communication is one-way and distorted. Teachers with a sound knowledge of a child's culture and environment will more likely understand the source and reasons for some student behaviors that appear odd or peculiar.

Children raised in slums are inadequately prepared for traditional schools. They appear to be physically inferior regarding the use of their eyes, ears, and other sensory organs. Positive social skills and habits of listening and observing are underdeveloped. Their attention span is short. They have not been encouraged to read or to ask questions about what they have seen and heard. When they enter school, they fail to measure up because they have not had the same opportunities as many of their classmates. Many become underachievers and school dropouts.

Facilitative teachers avoid bending the child to match the curriculum. Rather, they cultivate the talents and unique cultural characteristics of children. The facilitative teacher accepts the child as is and helps that child move on from that point. For example, one facilitative teacher noted that some of her underachieving children struggled with reading but knew the lyrics to popular music. It was highly valued and recognized in their homes. It was decided to set some of the primary reading books to music using popular songs. The children loved it and many learned to read through this approach. Some other teachers used neighborhood comic books as reading texts.

The facilitative teacher knows that culture can be a predisposition to learning. For example, psychologists in the Southwest have learned that child-rearing practices among the Navajo relate to learning. They have discovered that Navajo children only look their fathers in the eye when being disciplined. Thus, teachers who force a child to look directly at them ("Pay attention when I'm talking") would threaten a Navajo child. Navajo children also have a great deal of visual interest and appear to learn much better when instructed with visual aids.

The opposite seems to be true for most Spanish-American children. They are auditory learners who are able to conceptualize from abstract symbols through conversation. Teachers generally find spoken words effective with them, especially if a bi-lingual approach is used.

When teaching the culturally different it is important to preserve the self-respect and dignity of the student. The salesman in Meredith Wilson's *Music Man* lamented the fact that the new salesman would be ineffective because, "You gotta know the territory." Teacher, know your territory!

Chapter 3
The Facilitative Responses

This chapter is about communication in the classroom. More specifically, it is about teacher talk and how it influences the perceptions of students.

Past (e.g. Cohan, 1958) and current research (e.g. Cruickshank, 1986) draw attention to the relationship between certain teacher behaviors and the productive behaviors of students. These works indicate there is a relationship between the way a teacher is perceived by the students and the amount of self-initiated work they report doing. Consequently, the importance of teacher talk in the classroom goes beyond simply establishing good rapport with students. It is directly related to student achievement and success.

Current research indicates that some verbal responses tend to be perceived by students as more empathic, caring, warm, and person-centered than other responses. These responses that have a higher probability of creating a more facilitative or helping relationship than others are essential keys toward becoming a facilitative teacher.

Let's look at the case of Carl Willis again. Certainly, teacher talk had an important effect on his life. The following situations might have occurred in Carl Willis' school life. Each situation is described briefly and then followed by some possible responses that a teacher might make to Carl in an attempt to be helpful.

Imagine that you are the teacher. Read over the possible responses and rank in ascending order from 1 to 6 those you consider to be the most understanding and helpful. The wording may not be exactly what you would use, but disregard this factor as long as the response is the same type as you would favor.

1. Carl has been sent to you, a teaching team leader, because of a sudden reversal in the performance of his school work. It's known that he doesn't like to be in school. He says, "Why do you want to talk to me? I know I said I don't like school, but I haven't done anything wrong.... Besides, if I were back in the room, I could get my work done. And that's what you want to get after me for, isn't it?... Are you going to punish me?"

   a. You think you know, Carl, why I've called you in to talk with me.

   b. You don't like being here, Carl, and you're a little uneasy about talking with me.

   c. Carl, you're a lot like so many other boys your age who just don't like to talk with teachers. Things aren't always as bad as they might seem.

   d. Why are you so suspicious of me, Carl?

   e. Just relax, Carl. You need to think about some things with me. I think I can be of some help.

   f. You haven't given me much of a chance, Carl. You're suspicious of me because you expect to get punished.

2. A teacher has been pointing out some errors in homework within a small group of children. Carl reacts by saying, "Everything I do is wrong." (His eyes water a little.) "I just don't do anything right. All the other kids hear you talk about me and they joke about it. Because of you, nobody likes me.... I'm dumb, and you, you... always find my mistakes and tell everybody! (Tears again come to his eyes).

   a. I think you're saying that you don't like the way I talk with you about your school work.

   b. You don't want to admit to mistakes because you think that it will hurt your chances of being liked by the others.

   c. There's nothing wrong with making a mistake, Carl. Most of us make mistakes now and then.

   d. You're going to have a learn to be more objective, and not so sensitive, Carl.

    e. You're embarrassed and hurt because of what I said.

    f. What would have been a better way to talk with you about your work?

3. Carl says, "I wish I weren't in school. Sometimes it's okay, but most of the time I hate being here.... But, it's better than staying home and being "nagged." This place (school)... they expect so much. Things would be great if I could get away from here—anything is better than this.... I don't know.... I might just quit...."

    a. You're pretty unhappy now and imagine that things would be easier for you if you weren't in school.

    b. You think getting away from school is the answer because you could then be free to do want you want.

    c. If I understand you, you're saying that you've got a decision to make between staying in school or quitting.

    d. Things are looking bad for you right now, but I'm sure you'll find some way of working things out, and you'll feel better.

    e. What would you do if you quit school?

    f. You should talk with the school counselor about this, she has some interesting information you should see about dropouts.

4. Carl says that when he tries to study he can't concentrate. He thinks of all the things that need to be done. There are so many things to do. He says he might fail if something can't be done soon.

    a. Your mind wanders when you study and you're feeling the pressure of having to get things done soon.

    b. Well, as a student you're going to have to learn how to make better use of your time. One way is to develop a study schedule and learn to concentrate during that time.

    c. What do you think about when you're supposed to be studying?

    d. You think a lot about all the things that you have to do and getting them done on time.

    e. A lot of students have trouble settling down to work at first; but, they learn how and you can too.

f. You know, Carl, thinking about other things and everything that needs to be done is one way of avoiding what has to be done - the actual studying or reading.

The kind of talk that takes place in any conversation is important. Every response makes an impact on listeners. This impact invariably affects the general perception of the talker by the listeners. From what a talker says, listeners gain an impression and they use it, not only to formulate their own responses, but to reach an understanding of the relationship they have with this person. Therefore, it is important to understand the probable impact that certain responses will have on individuals.

From studies of verbal behavior in counseling, psychotherapy, and teaching, there emerges a set of responses that can be categorized from the least facilitative to the most facilitative. These are:

1. focusing on feelings (most facilitative)
2. clarifying and summarizing
3. questioning
4. reassuring and supporting
5. analyzing and interpreting
6. advising and evaluating (least facilitative)

While all of these responses might be considered facilitative responses at one time or another, they are ranked as above because of their probable effect in building a helping relationship.

Now, let's see how facilitative you were in responding to Carl Willis in the four situations. Remember, you wanted him to perceive you as helpful and understanding. The six responses are placed in order of least facilitative (6) to most facilitative (1) in Table 1. Check your answers with the table.

Using Table 1, you can see how each of the six responses in the four situations has been designated. For example, if you tended to favor responses b, a, and d in the first situation, though not necessarily in that order, then you were selecting high facilitative responses. These same four situations were also presented to you in an open-ended fashion in Chapter 1. Turn back and check your original responses. Were you favoring the least or the most facilitative responses? Let's see if we can gain a better understanding of these responses and how they can be helpful in our relationship with others. They are presented in order of most facilitative (1— focusing on feelings) to least facilitative (6—advising and evaluating).

Table 1
The Case of Carl Willis (Part I)

Reflecting or Understanding of Feeling	Clarifying or Summarizing	Reassuring or Questioning	Interpreting or Supporting	Advising or Analyzing	Evaluating
(1)	(2)	(3)	(4)	(5)	(6)
Most facilitative					Least facilitative

Situation

1.	b	a	d	c	f	e
2.	e	a	f	c	b	d
3.	a	c	e	d	b	f
4.	a	d	c	e	f	b

Focusing on Feelings

A feeling-focused response conveys to students that we are "reading" what they are experiencing. It is a reflection of understanding. It communicates accurately that we know how they are feeling about themselves at this time. For example:

> *You're disappointed, Jane, with your math score.*
> *You're feeling confused about the assignment.*
> *It seems that you are really tired and feeling low on energy.*

The reflection or understanding of feeling statement can be a difficult response to learn. It demands that we be empathic listeners. It requires that we listen beyond mere words for the feelings. It calls for us to reflect these feelings to the person.

Facilitative teachers often verbalize what they think their students are feeling. This involves more than a restatement of words and should not be confused with other responses that focus on the general ideas that are being expressed. Nor should it be confused with an interpretation, which tends to explain why a person might be doing something. Rather, it gives priority to feelings that go with the words and behaviors that are being seen and heard.

To begin a sentence with "You feel..." does not necessarily mean that you will focus on someone's feeling. For example, "I feel that you would make a good president" is not a feeling-focused response. It is an opinion. We must go beyond the words to the feeling within the speaker in order to get credit for a feeling-focused response. Sometimes it can be helpful to ask yourself: How would I feel if I were to say something like that? Or, how would I have to feel to do something like that? After answering these questions, we may have some insight into the student's feeling. If this seems to be accurate or compatible with what we are sensing from the student, then this feeling could be stated. Remember, however, that we can distort what some people say. Our own value systems and perceptions, at times, prevent us from being sensitive to another person's feelings.

No one can talk without feelings. All of us feel something at all times. Both verbal and nonverbal cues tell us how a person feels. For our purposes, feelings can be categorized into 1) pleasant feelings or 2) unpleasant feelings. Sometimes we hear both kinds of feelings when a person is talking. Look at the feeling words that follow:

Pleasant	Unpleasant
enjoyment	defeated
satisfied	suspicious
excited	doubtful
loved	threatened
happy	offended
contented	disgusted
delighted	guarded
proud	angry
hopeful	hateful
accepted	rejected
calm	cramped
pleasant	tense
warm	worried
close	troubled
strong	shocked
optimistic	depressed
fascinated	distant
joyful	annoyed
pleased	disappointed
cheerful	pained
stimulated	abused
refreshed	uneasy
rejoicing	uncomfortable
trusting	gloomy
confident	sad
secure	irritated
interested	tired
needing	flexible
powerful	fearful
relieved	defensive

When listening to a person talk, we might ask ourselves: Do I hear unpleasant feelings or pleasant feelings, or both? Think about the feeling words that might best describe what is heard or sensed from a student. If we hear pleasant feelings, then we might say something like:

You're excited about studying the castles of Europe.

You were feeling confident before the test.

You're delighted with the idea that your parents might be moving soon.

You're really pleased with your project.

The customs of the oriental cultures fascinate you.

On the other hand, if we hear some unpleasantness, we might say:

It was a painful experience for you.

You're really angry

The results disappointed you.

You're feeling discouraged and wonder what's the use.

I hear a lot of sadness when you speak of your brother.

It can be so irritating to you.

Maybe we are hearing both pleasant and unpleasant feelings. Or, perhaps even some ambivalence. We might then say something like:

French is challenging to you, but you feel awkward just starting.

The first experience disappointed you, but you're encouraged now about the new possibilities.

You're excited about going to college, but afraid you might not be as good a student as people say you are.

You were feeling so optimistic and then suddenly when you found you weren't chosen, things looked gloomy.

You're proud, yet skeptical.

You are interested in chemistry, but afraid you'll fail.

Suppose a seventh grade girl told you bluntly that she hated having to ride a bus to school. In this case a facilitative teacher might have focused on her feelings by saying:

It irritates you at times to have to ride the bus. (Gets to the basic feeling).

Or,

Riding the bus isn't much fun for you. (Captures the feeling tone and mirrors back the overall picture that is presented).

After responding to feelings, try not to rush in with other statements. Let the response and impact take full effect. Pause a little, giving the person an opportunity to experience your interest and understanding. More often than not, if you are reasonably accurate, the student will unconsciously nod (as if to say, "Yes, that's right" or "Thanks for hearing me") and talk some more. It is a pleasant experience for both speaker and listener.

It should be noted that when you respond to people's feelings, your statement could be rejected. Sometimes it's difficult for students to acknowledge feelings. They may even deny them. However, it is important that your response be made because it says you are trying to understand what the person is experiencing. Feeling focused responses communicate that you are not only listening to words, but that you are listening to that special part of the person which makes up those words. A reflection of feeling is almost always facilitative because the student will probably correct you if you have misunderstood. Even the attempt puts "chips in the bank."

Learning to tune in on a person's feelings and reflect them accurately takes practice, practice, and more practice! It does not come easily to most of us because we have not had many adult models to learn from while we were children, or even now as adults.

Hiding feelings is often a step on the road to ineffective learning and even emotional disturbance. When people retreat from others and experience dehumanizing relationships, inefficient learning climates are created. This may occur in schools or other life situations. Consequently, many dysfunctioning individuals and poor learners are likely products of poor school and home relationships. The facilitative teacher accepts part of the responsibility for reversing the factors which impede positive personal growth and achievement.

Unfortunately, the feeling-focused response is used infrequently in the classroom. Experimental studies and classroom observations reveal that teachers respond to children's feelings (either positively or negatively) less than one out of a thousand times.

Is this because there is no time for feeling? Is it because teachers believe that feelings are not an important part of the learning process? Is it because teachers give student feelings low priority in building relationships? Or, is it because many teachers have not learned the skill of responding to someone's feelings?

In order to help you answer these questions, please complete Worksheet 1 at this time.

Worksheet 1

Feeling-focused Responses

Please record your responses below.

Example A:

Student:
Maybe if I had worked harder, I could have been in the advanced math group.

Your feeling-focused response:

Example B:

Student:
I made a C in English and now my parents won't let me go with my friends to visit the old temples next week.

Your feeling-focused response:

Example C:

Student:
My teacher, Mrs. Boxwell, said I was the best-behaved student in the class!

Your feeling-focused response:

Example D:

Student:
I had a lot of fun on my vacation, but coming back to school has been tough.

Your feeling-focused response:

Sample responses to Worksheet 1 are found in the Appendix.

Clarifying and Summarizing

Any response that is an attempt to acknowledge the content of what a person has said, or to identify the most significant ideas that seem to have been stated, can be termed a clarifying or summarizing response. Such a statement is helpful when there is some doubt as to whether you're really following the student's thinking and feeling. In this case, a clarification statement is a simple way of checking out what has been heard. In other situations, the clarifying or summarizing response is deliberately used to help students "hear" what they have said.

When there is a lot of talk in a spontaneous and fast conversation, you cannot expect to understand or grasp everything. Yet, an attempt to let students know that you are interested in following what is being said can help facilitate communication.

The clarification statement involves "fresh" (or new) words. It is an attempt to simplify or focus what has been said. Clarifying or summarizing statements focus on the ideas or content of the discussion. This emphasis tends to separate these responses from feeling-focused responses. Clarifying or summarizing responses can give you some "wiggle room." Consider the following:

If I hear you correctly, you are telling me that....

You seem to be saying that....

If I am following you, you're saying....

Correct me if I'm wrong, but you're thinking....

Let me see if I understand what you are saying.... You said....

Let's see, your aim is to....

Facilitative teachers use clarifying or summarizing statements when they want to check out a student's thoughts. These statements have a way of reassuring students that they are being listened to and heard. Other examples include:

I think you're telling me that this has happened before.

Let me see now, you're saying that cheating, as long as you don't get caught,. is okay.

Let's see, you said... and... and....

Remember the seventh grade girl described in the previous section who said, "I hate to ride the bus to school;

I have to get up so early and then wait and wait for the bus.... Then it's so noisy. Just about anything would be better than riding that old bus."

A *facilitative* teacher might have said any of the following:

1. *You don't like riding the bus to school.* **(Clarifying and Summarizing:** An attempt to clarify the central theme of the child's words).

2. *A lot of things make you wish you weren't riding the bus.* **(Clarifying and Summarizing:** Ignores feelings, but generally clarified the child's words in a short statement).

3. *It seems to me that from what you've said, riding the bus makes school unpleasant for you.* **(Clarifying and Summarizing:** Attempts to get at feelings, but there is no feeling word, only the conclusion that school is unpleasant. The opening qualifying phrase gives the child "wiggle room.")

Clarifying and summarizing responses are not difficult to learn and use but they are not used as much as they could be. Worksheet 2 is intended to help you develop your clarifying and summarizing response skills.

Worksheet 2

Clarifying and Summarizing

Read the responses below and write your clarifying or summarizing responses to each example.

Example A:

Student:
I want to travel so that I can meet new and interesting people.

Your clarification response:

Example B:

Student:
I don't like biology lab because of the smell and the dissected animals lying around.

Your clarification response:

Example C:

Student:
I just moved to this school two weeks ago and I'm already behind in my subjects.

Your clarification response:

Sample responses to Worksheet 2 are found in the Appendix.

Questioning

The art of questioning has often been thought of as the central part of the educational process. A lot has been written about how to ask questions. In fact, entire books have been written about questioning strategies. Student textbooks almost always conclude chapters or lessons with a series of questions, and these questions are frequently followed by more questions asked by the classroom teacher.

The school curriculum is planned to help students analyze and synthesize information. With an increasing trend toward an inquiry approach to learning, educators are arming themselves with a host of questions that they believe will stimulate students. Yet, over 90 percent of the questions that teachers ask deal only with recall of cognitive knowledge.

There is no doubt that questions are a valuable tool in the learning process. However, teachers tend to ask too many questions. Bombarding students with questions can be a frightening experience for them. It has been compared, by one student, to facing a prosecuting attorney who asks questions in order to trap witnesses. Some questions can make people feel uneasy and put them on the defensive, while others encourage people to talk about themselves and their ideas.

A question can be used to obtain information, stimulate further discussion, or to query an individual regarding a particular matter. Teachers assume that a student will benefit by answering a question and developing a point of view. Questions may also open up new areas for discussion. Facilitative questions encourage the sharing of information.

Students try to give a response that will satisfy the person asking a question. Sometimes this can lead to a quick question and answer pattern. If such a pattern occurs often, then open and spontaneous interaction is usually impeded. Discussion seems stifled and boring.

Questions can determine the scope of the information that is being collected, the depth of that information, and the pace of the discussion. But, most important, they affect personal and teaching relationships.

Teachers see cross-examination procedures as an essential part of their trade. It is assumed that questioning procedures will be productive and that probing questions lead to problem solving and indepth learning. However, students are also lead to believe, concurrently, that whoever is asking the questions also has the answers.

If a student has a problem and a teacher asks a lot of questions, there may be the expectation that, since the teacher now has the information, the teacher should solve the problem or make a decision. Students reason that if teachers cannot solve the problem, then why did they ask all the questions? This may be perfectly acceptable in cases where cognitive learning is based upon confirmed information and facts. But, it can lead to a dead end street when there is no easy answer or correct response.

Obviously, teachers should question their students. They ask questions as part of learning. Moreover, questions can play an important role in any interpersonal relationship. Here are some things that might be kept in mind:

1. What is the purpose of a question?
2. What kinds of questions are available?
3. What impact will a question have on the student/teacher relationship?
4. What alternative response might be used instead of a question?

For our purposes questions will be divided into two types: *open* and *closed* questions.

Open and Closed Questions

The open question encourages students to develop their answers. The closed question, on the other hand, is structured for only a yes or no responses. It doesn't tend to elicit an indepth response. Look at the following examples.

> Do you like the notion of going to boarding school next year? (closed)
> What do you think about going to boarding school next year? (open)

> Did you like reading this section? (closed)
> How did you feel about this section? (open)

> Are you ready for the test? (closed)
> What can we do to get you ready for the test? (open)

> Do you understand the International Baccalaureate Curriculum? (closed)
> What can you tell me about the International Baccalaureate Curriculum? (open)

The open question invites students to answer from their own perceptual fields. A closed question is narrow and forces students to answer in terms of the teacher's perceptual field. The open question solicits a wide range of thoughts and feelings. The closed question tends to seek cold facts. Consider the following questions, some of which seem to be open but are not.

> You don't like this school, do you? (closed)
> What is it that you don't like about this school? (open)
>
> Is this the part that's confusing to you? (closed)
> What part is confusing to you? (open)

Of all questions, open-ended questions are the most facilitative for student growth and learning. While closed questions might be used at times to gain specific information that will help clarify a situation, open-ended questions give students the most room to discover their innermost feelings and thoughts about a matter.

The open-ended question is more person-centered because it keeps the questioner from getting ahead of the respondent. Person-centered questions enable us to follow the student's thinking, rather than have the student follow ours.

The "why" question is a type of open question that deserves special attention. Most people don't know why they do the things they do. Do people who are abusing drugs really know why they started? Do persons who tell dirty jokes know why it is fun to tell them? Do children know why they have the friends they have? Why questions often have a negative connotation in our society.

While there is probably an explanation behind behavior, it is doubtful that a "why" question will help discover it. These questions have a way of making people uneasy. They require people to explain themselves, to be accountable, to come up with a reasonable link or connection. They often force people to rationalize.

Effective counselors and teachers have learned to be cautious in the use of "why" questions. When such questions are posed, individuals tend to become defensive and feel pressure to "explain away" their behaviors, without seeking changes.

Please complete "Worksheet 3" for practice in using alternative questions.

Worksheet 3
Open-ended Questions

Here are some typical statements from students, followed by closed questions. Read each statement along with the closed question that follows and then substitute your open-ended questions below for all three (3) examples.

Example 1:

Student:
Maybe if I had worked harder at my reading last year, I could have been in the advanced reading group.

Teacher:
Are you going to try for it this year?

Your open-ended question:

Example 2:

Student:
I hate math.

Teacher:
Do you study very hard?

Your open-ended question:

Example 3:

Student:
Chorus tryouts are next week and I'm scared.

Teacher:
Why are you scared?

Your open-ended question:

Sample responses to Worksheet 3 are found in the Appendi.

The Least Facilitative Responses

We know that some responses tend to be perceived by students as more empathic, caring, warm, and person-centered. They have a higher probability of facilitating students to think more about their ideas and feelings. They provide a tone which fosters a helping relationship, eliciting the conditions of warmth, understanding, respect, regard, and so forth. Skill in the use of these responses is the key to becoming a facilitative teacher.

The talking that takes place in any conversation is important since every response makes some kind of impact on the participants. Responses to each other invariably affect general perceptions, attitudes, and degree of comfort. Impressions are formed which, in turn, influence other responses, choice of topics, and what will be shared.

While all responses, at one time or another, might be facilitative, they are ranked from high to low because of their probable effects in establishing a helping relationship. We have examined three of the most facilitative (1-3), now let's look briefly at some others that are considered less facilitative (4-6).

> Reassuring and supporting
> Analyzing and interpreting
> Advising and evaluating

Reassuring and Supporting

Reassurance or support involves statements which are intended to tell students that we believe in them, their ability to meet situations, and their potential for solving problems. We want to tell them that we have confidence that they will be successful. It is supposed to be a pat on the back, intended to help them keep going.

Unfortunately, reassuring or supporting responses can also imply that individuals need not feel as they do. That is, there is a tendency to dismiss feelings as being normal or common and the person is told in so many words not to be concerned. For example:

> *Don't worry, everyone feels like that on occasion.*
>
> *You don't have to feel that way because everything's going to turn out okay.*
>
> *You know, in that respect you're not much different from kids your age.*
>
> *Oh, all mothers are like that.*

I felt like that once, too.

You are a lot like a boy I know—Willis.

Things always look bad at this time of the year, but it will turn out okay.

I know exactly how you feel.

It has the same effect on me, too.

Why, Helen, you're not fat. Besides, there's nothing wrong with you that two years of growth won't take care of.

The reassuring or supportive kind of statement is the second most popular response used by teachers. Only advice and evaluation are used more frequently. Many teachers believe that a supportive statement can encourage a student to do better. "I am building the student's self-confidence," is a common rationalization for this statement. But, it doesn't usually strike the student this way. Despite efforts to reduce the apparent anxiety or intense feelings, the message comes through telling people not to feel as they do. It denies feelings. It does not communicate acceptance, respect, or understanding.

Philosophical truisms or Pollyanna-like statements have a similar effect. They intend to offer encouragment and hope. "It's always dark just before the sunshines." Too many times, such truisms and "everything will turn out okay" statements are perceived as a lack of interest or understanding. In most cases, innermost feelings are ignored.

Sometimes supporting and reassuring statements create a negative effect because they come from a seemingly superior position. When we give reassurance or support, it frequently implies that we can see into the future and that our positive estimations will be correct. They can count on us.

One teacher said to a young girl, "Now, Alice didn't mean to do that. She was just trying to help you. You shouldn't be angry with her. Things will be better pretty soon." When the child heard this, the teacher sounded very calm, soothing, and reassuring. It sounded good—for the moment. But after the teacher left, the child sensed that her feelings of anger and hurt had not been recognized as true or important. The child sensed that she had not been understood at all. She still felt angry and hurt. Moreover, when Alice continued to pick on her, she concluded, "Why should I go to the teacher again, she was wrong." This teacher wasn't seen as understanding by the young girl.

Analyzing and Interpreting

Some teachers think that they can be helpful by analyzing (and subsequently "explaining") a situation for a student. Perhaps this response gained its popularity from the theory that there is always a logical reason why people do things. Look at these responses:

Don't you see, your teacher is like your father. They both are authority figures and they trigger off rebellion in you.

You were thinking that Mrs. Jones is a lot like Mr. Brown and that she wouldn't want to hear you tell about your trip.

Your unhappiness stems from a lack of success in school.

Jane said that she didn't want you on her team and that's why you left the playground.

You sit there and don't participate in class because you're afraid that you will fail.

The reason you dislike this assignment is because it makes you think.

In all of these examples, the intent is to explain, analyze, or interpret the student's behavior. Sometimes an effort is made to connect one event to another, in the hope that this will give the person some insight. Analyzing or interpreting responses try to give meaning to a situation but they usually end up telling people what they might or ought to think.

How do you feel when someone tries to analyze or interpret your behavior? Chances are you don't like it. Most of us dislike the idea that another person might know more about ourselves than we do.

Sometimes a person making the interpretation is accurate, but most of the time that person is only guessing. Too many times an analytic statement tends to be a textbook interpretation, or a general analysis. For example, "When you threw the eraser in class, Charles, you wanted everyone to give you attention, and that's the reason you continue to act up." This might be accurate. But again, the teacher may only be guessing as to what really motivated Charles. Maybe someone threw the eraser at him first and he felt the urge to retaliate or to prove his physical strength.

Have you ever had a person say in so many words, "Do you know why you did that? Well, I've been reading about that and let me tell you...." If you could remember your reaction at the time, there's a good chance that you coldly withdrew. People don't like to be seen as an entry in a textbook. While the amateur analyst is hoping for an "ah, ha," many times that person gets an "uh, uh," or "nope" because such statements provoke defensiveness.

One danger in making an interpretation is that we often project our own attitudes, values, and feelings onto others. It emphasizes our personal interpretation of the world rather than the other person's perception. Fortunately, this is not a popular response among teachers, unless they have been told to "counsel" a child.

Playing psychologist or counselor causes many people to increase the number of analytic or interpretive responses in their work. In actuality, effective counselors and therapists no longer rely heavily on these types of statements to facilitate personal growth. Rather than attempting to explain the reasons behind student behaviors, the facilitative teacher is interested in helping them become more aware of what they are experiencing.

Advising and Evaluating

Traditionally, teachers are people in authority. From their lofty positions, teachers judge and evaluate student work and frequently make arbitrary decisions as to how students are performing and how they might improve their skills. Many teachers also create the image that they are always right, that their ideas are the most valuable ones, and that their opinions and ideas should not be questioned. Because teachers are older, have probably studied more, and usually have more experience than most of their students, they sometimes think they are in a position to evaluate, make judgments, and give advice.

When teachers stand in front of their classrooms throughout the day, dispensing information and advice to students, they are probably not at their facilitative best. Moreover, in that position they are prone to use more low facilitative responses.

Facilitative teachers are more concerned with what the student is thinking and feeling than simply giving information and advice. They try to avoid being seen as judge and executor. Rather, they create opportunities to use more high facilitative than low facilitative responses.

Advising or evaluating are responses that indicate a judgment of relative goodness, appropriateness, effectiveness, or rightness within the teacher's own value structure. An advising or evaluating response somehow implies what the student might or ought to do. Here are some examples:

Don't drop geometry, you can use it to get a better job someday.

Instead of arguing, try to see your parents' point of view.

When you have a problem like that, you should talk with one of the school counselors. They are trained to help you.

If you'd study more, your parents wouldn't be so upset with you.

If I were you, I'd look at the positive side.

Show Mr. Jones some of your homework and then he will know that you've been studying.

You'd better start getting good grades or you won't make it to college.

What you need to do is see Mr. Tobias, the principal. He's not as unfair as you might think.

Go to the library and get a book on the subject. Skim the major headings and you can get an idea for a term paper.

One of the best things to do now is to talk with your teachers and find out why they ignore you.

Responses that give advice are easily identified because they tell people how to behave or what to do. Unfortunately, while most teachers are trying to give helpful advice, there is the likelihood the advice is a projection of the teacher's needs, problems, or values. This can be easily seen in the statement, "If I were you...." Students might even follow the advice and find that it was not valid for them.

Notice how such statements try to influence a student's thinking.

You can....
The best solution is....
One good way is....
Why don't you....
You should....
You ought to....
I think....
You need....
If I were you....
If you would....
The thing to do is....
The best way is....
If you don't, then....

In some form or another advice is received and given by almost everyone every day. Listen to any conversation, whether in a business or a social setting, and notice how often people offer advice when an individual expresses concern about something.

When advice is relevant, logical, and practical, it can be very helpful. This is particularly true if it is offered at an appropriate time—a time when it is viewed as a suggestion rather than as a command. For example, administrators can fall into the trap of giving advice when a student needs to be disciplined. Students are usually defensive at this time and unreceptive to any advice that might be given. They might even argue more in order to maintain their individuality. Facilitative responses might first be given and later followed by advice, if time permits. In this case, the students are more likely to listen to suggestions and receive advice.

Counselors and psychotherapists recognize that advice-giving shifts the responsibility for solving the problem from the person to the counselor or therapist. Such an approach may limit the person's opportunity to make changes and rob that person of the satisfaction of a personal resolution. Facilitative teachers recognize similar implications for their work with students.

The "discovery method" of teaching is valued because it encourages children to accept responsibility for learning. Lecturing is contradictory to discovery learning. Similarly, advice-giving is contradictory to students solving their own problems.

Another problem of giving advice and making evaluations is that it is often perceived as threatening, since advice and evaluation are sometimes a form of criticism. Consequently, this response category frequently produces hesitation, resistance, rejection, and inaction in students.

Still another problem of advising and evaluating is that it tends to disrupt the flow of communication. When teachers project their own value systems through judging, evaluating, or giving advice, a student may begin to think defensively.

For example, the student may think:

> *He won't like what I'm going to say now.*
> *She's going to think that I am....*
> *He wants me to....*
> *She won't understand me.*
> *I should... if I want him to like me.*

When advice and evaluation are used to motivate students, there is a tendency to feel that certain expectations must be met if they are to be of value. There is the thought that they must continue to produce for teachers or parents in order to gain their attention, acceptance, and respect. When overused, such responses also create a dependency.

If you are doubting the effect that advice or evaluation has upon individuals, check it out by giving someone some "good" advice and then notice the person's reaction. Most likely the first few words uttered will be, "*Yes*, but..." or, "That's a good idea, *however*..." or, take note of your own feelings when someone gives you advice or evaluates you.

There is no way around it, advice and evaluation must be rated as low facilitators of communication and low in establishing a helping relationship. This is not to say that advice or evaluation should never be given. All of us have benefited from advice at one time or another. When advice is timely and relevant, it has positive impact. Unfortunately, we usually rush in with advice or offer evaluations before we know what the other person is really saying.

Rather than give advice or make a judgment, a facilitative teacher tries to open the flow of communication by first thinking, "I need to know how students see the situation, rather than sharing my own value judgments at this time." A facilitative teacher tends to think, "I can best help students by exploring the situation, including alternatives and consequences from their point of view rather than telling them what is right or wrong." Or, "I can be of help by encouraging students to examine their own ideas further and by clarifying situations."

Advice and evaluation are rated as the least facilitative of responses. Ironically, they are the most popular responses used in classrooms or individual conferences. However, facilitative teachers also realize that giving advice is frequently used because it is often expedient, even though other responses are more productive. Torn between many events that take place in a classroom, some teachers think there is not enough time to be facilitative.

Using the High Facilitative Responses

To test the validity of the rankings of facilitative responses, studies were conducted in elementary and secondary schools. In one study, three discussion leaders were asked to meet with six groups of eighth grade students. Each of the leaders were assigned to two groups which were matched according to age, sex, academic achievement, and general interest in school. Each leader met with the two groups on two occasions. In the first meeting all groups discussed "likes and dislikes about school." In the second meeting the topic was "pet peeves about adults."

In most respects the groups were highly similar. However, each leader was trained and then instructed to respond with the most facilitative responses (feelings, clarifying, summarizing, open questions) in one group, and the least facilitative responses (advice, evaluation, interpretation, reassurance) in the other group. Tape recordings were made to assure that each group was receiving the assigned responses from the group leaders.

After the two meetings, students in all six groups were asked to complete a relationship inventory. Results of the study were conclusive. Those students who were in the groups where discussion leaders responded with high facilitative responses tended to perceive the leaders as more empathic, caring, interested, and respectful, among other positive helping characteristics. Conversely, students in the other groups rated their leaders considerably lower on these characteristics.

If you want to be more facilitative, then you will want to learn different responses and the probable impact that responses have on students. You will want to increase the use of the most facilitative responses, practicing them until they become an integrated part of your teaching style. If you increase the use of the high facilitative responses in your relationships with others, learning and personal growth can facilitated and you will enjoy your work more.

Research has shown there is a high probability when the frequency of the high facilitative responses is increased, then students are more likely to perceive us as warm, caring, interested, and helping persons. It is important to note, however, genuineness is not cited. Genuineness is the part of us that shows we are real, not phony. Genuineness says we are honest and not attempting to fool someone else. When a person is playing a role, there is a high probability the "playing" will prevent the person from being one's real and most effective self.

As you begin to increase the use of the high facilitative responses in your work, especially focusing on feelings and clarifying, you may experience some awkward moments. The high facilitative responses described in this book are not common classroom responses and they can, at times, appear to be out-of-place. Many teachers who are beginning to use high facilitative responses report

they feel uncomfortable at first. They sometimes feel less than genuine because the responses feel forced and do not flow easily. Interestingly enough, our experience suggests that students will not
perceive you as phony or weird. To the contrary, they tend to see
you as taking time to listen to them and trying to be understanding.

These responses, like many other things that are new, require practice. With practice they become an integrated part of one's personality. Then it takes less concentration and the responses flow
naturally as a part of being a facilitative person.

The game of golf provides us with an excellent analogy. If you
have tried the game, or perhaps witnessed it on television, then you
know that there are many hints which a professional might give to
someone who wants to play the game. You might be shown the correct grip and then told to keep your eyes of the ball. In addition,
you might be shown how to position your body, to move your hips,
to hold your hands in the aloft position, and then, "Remember, let
it fly and finish high." Wow! All that to remember. No wonder
some of us don't have smooth golf swings or play the game well.

If we observe closely, there are several differences between the
golf swings of great golfers. They are all beyond the stage of "Keep
your eye on the ball, keep your left elbow in tight," and all the
other little suggestions. As professionals they have integrated the
techniques into their game styles. Because of many hours of practice, they no longer feel awkward in hitting a golf ball; rather, they
sense when their swing is correct and when it is not. On occasion
they have to focus on one aspect of their game or get some coach-
ing or help from someone else.

While all of the professional golfers have their own way of approaching a golf game, just as all facilitative teachers will have
their own individual styles of teaching, they all know the purpose
of the game. All of them also know how to use the tools that are
available.

As facilitative teachers, we want to learn the high facilitative
responses and integrate them into our teaching styles. As we
become more professional as facilitators and teachers, we will
sense which "tool" to use at the right time. There are times when
advice will be most appropriate. At other times, it would be much
like using a driver to get out of a sand trap. It could work and it
might be effective, but the probability of success is much lower
than if a more appropriate response were used.

If a facilitative relationship between students and teachers is not present, then students—and teachers—will pull back into their shells. They are like a tortoise who, when threatened, will not stick it's head out. Words never penetrate their hard shells or enter into their perceptual fields. There will be times when we will want to offer advice, information, or directions, but will first want to make sure the student is "out of the shell." We can do this with the help of facilitative responses. As students experience a relatively non-threatening teaching relationship, they are more apt to "stick their necks out and risk more." They are more likely to consider the alternative suggestions and methods that we may offer in helping them.

Now, complete worksheet 4.

Worksheet 4

A Summary of the Facilitative Responses

Listed below are six sample student/teacher interactions that have been presented in the previous sections. You have two tasks for each case. First, identify the type of facilitative response made by the teacher in each situation. Second, write out the alternative type of facilitative response.

Sample 1

Student:
I never realized I learned so much in your class. My test score is better than I expected.

Teacher:
You seem surprised.

Type of response given:

Your open-ended questioning response would be (Begin your question with How... or What...):

Sample 2

Student:
These test results show that I should be an accountant. That's what I want to be. Does that mean I'll be good at it?

Teacher:
(smiling) *Anyone can be good at anything if they try hard enough.*

Type of response given:

Your clarifying or summarizing response would be (Restate the content in fresh words):

Sample 3

Student:
I don't like our human growth and development class; they ask questions I'm embarrassed to answer.

Teacher:
You think some questions are too personal.

Type of response given:

Your open-ended questioning response would be (Begin your question with How... or What...):

Sample 4

Student:
(To another student) *You're so stupid, you don't even know what's good for you.*

Teacher:
You insulted him because he wouldn't take your advice.

Type of response given:

Your feeling-focused response would be (Think about how the student must be feeling and reflect it back without a "because"):

Sample 5

Student:
What do you mean when you say I can't do that?

Teacher:
You should have listened, then you'd know what I mean.

Type of response given:

Your clarifying and summarizing response would be (Rephrase the content without being a parrot.):

Sample 6

Student:
I can't figure out the difference between these two graphs.

Teacher:
Study them a little longer and you'll figure it out.

Type of response given:

Your feeling-focused response (Pleasant or unpleasant feeling?):

Sample responses to Worksheet 4 are found in the Appendix.

Chapter 4
Facilitating Classroom Discussion

The three high facilitative responses discussed in the preceding sections can be used to improve teacher-student relationships, as well as learning and personal relationships between students. While many responses might be considered facilitative at a given time, open-ended questions, clarifying and summarizing, and feeling-focused responses are considered most facilitative.

As you respond to students in facilitative ways, the helping relationship between you and your students will be enhanced. As students experience personal interest, caring, and understanding, they become more open to exploring ideas, following directions, and receiving suggestions.

Some teachers have said, "If only I could work with that student on a one-to-one basis... I'm sure that I could make a difference." However, teachers work, more often than not, with students through classroom groups. Effective teachers can establish a positive working relationship with each student and, at the same time, create a positive group experience for all students who are working together in a classroom.

Facilitative teachers know how to manage groups. They are aware of the forces which result from people working in groups and can use group dynamics to enhance learning. Knowing how to respond to students in a group and to lead a group discussion, of course, are among the most important skills that a classroom teacher can have.

As a teacher you will work with several students at one time. Your students will form working relationships with you and their classmates. Everyone is performing in front of others. Everyone is watching, listening and learning from each other. The interaction among you and your students is what creates the learning climate.

The pace at which a discussion moves can make a difference in whether a discussion is productive or not. If a class discussion or lesson moves too rapidly, some students feel "lost" or perhaps ignored. Facilitative teachers control the pace of their classroom activities and discussions through what they say and their choice of activities. Let's take a closer look at two more facilitative responses.

To this point, three high facilitative responses have been emphasized. These three responses (feeling-focused, clarifying and summarizing, open-ended questions) can be used with individuals or groups. Two other responses can be added to these to help you become even more facilitative when leading a group discussion: (1) linking, and (2) simple acknowledgement.

The Linking Response

You can "link" students together through your observations and comments. Linking responses are statements that accentuate relationships by pairing information, similarities and differences, from one person to another.

Information in this context is broadly defined and includes both cognitive and affective characteristics. More specifically, the cognitive focus is on the general content, ideas, and events of the story that is being told. The affective focus gives attention to feelings or emotions. Although "linking" may be on the basis of either a similarity or a difference among students, most teachers prefer to look for how students are alike. Moreover, it is possible to "link" several students by naming them as you draw attention to how they share the same ideas, events, or feelings.

As you read the following examples, ask yourself whether the linking has cognitive or affective emphasis.

Example A

Student 1:
My favorite sport is tennis.

Student 2:
I like baseball the best.

Teacher: *You both seem to be interested in sports, especially where you're hitting a ball. (Linking content)*

Example B

James:
I hate studying geography and my test score shows it.

Jeff:
I don't much care about it either but I got a pretty good score on the test.

Teacher:
Studying geography is not a favorite subject for either of you. (Linking content)

Example C

Rachel:
Mom will be mad when she sees my English grade.

Bill:
My older brother's going to be really mad. He's been helping me, but I didn't do well on this test.

Teacher:
Rachel, both you and Bill are worried about how your family is going to react to your test scores. (Linking feelings and content)

Example D

James:
I sure hope I make the team... but I don't know....

Derek:
Yeah, we'd all like to know who's going to make it. It's going to be tough.

Teacher:
Derek and James, you both seem worried. (Linking feelings)

Example E

Gloria:
I would love to go to college and become a nurse.

Stephanie:
College sounds good, but I want to be a veterinarian and work with animals.

Teacher:
Both of you are thinking about the field of medicine and about college. (Linking content)

In the last case the teacher attempted to pair "content" or "topic" by using the term "medicine." However, suppose that the teacher had heard some feelings expressed by the same two students and then said the following:

Teacher:
You both talk about the medical field with a lot of enthusiasm. It's exciting to think about it.

Now the teacher has linked them with feeling and content. There will be times when you will want to link only content or only feelings, and times when you will link both. It is the act of linking— what people are saying and experiencing—that makes the positive difference. Linking adds to the group's feelings of togetherness and creates group cohesiveness in a classroom. It also shows that you are aware of relationships among the students in class.

In the examples above, the teacher's response tried to include student names, which emphasizes the link and personalizes the bond. The use of names is especially effective and needed in large groups, such as a classroom group.

Simple Acknowledgement

The simple acknowledgement response is a way of getting closure to a person's statement or idea and, at the same time, recognizing the contribution. Here are some examples:

"Thank you for sharing that."
"Alright...."
"Thanks."
"I appreciate your telling us your ideas."
"Okay...."

This kind of response thanks a person for participating. But, it does not encourage the person to continue talking at that moment. There is, in a sense, an ending to the person's participation for that time. The acknowledgement produces closure. Such statements can help shape the kind and amount of conversation.

Suppose a student discussion has digressed and comments are no longer relevant or pertinent to the topic. The teacher might say something like, "Okay... that sounds like it's really important to you. I can see that. Right now, however, let's move on to...." This acknowledges a student's contribution and at the same time brings closure. It doesn't leave the person hanging, but it does allow you to refocus the discussion. By such simple acknowledgements you let students know that you've heard them and are ready to move on, perhaps in a new direction.

The acknowledgement response avoids a "plop experience." This can occur when someone says something and then someone else begins talking with out reference to what the first person said. The first speaker can experience a void, a feeling of having been ignored, or get the impression that the idea or remarks were unimportant. Even if the idea is not exactly accurate or pertinent, people want their contribution to be acknowledged. A simple acknowledgement response on your part will often suffice.

Thus, you can use six basic high-facilitative responses to lead a group discussion. When used in various combinations, you will find that students participate more and that you will have more confidence in leading the group. The high-facilitative responses can help keep students on task or help them digress a little and explore an idea in depth. They give attention to personal interests and needs, as well as academic matters. They encourage students by personalizing the learning experience.

Worksheet 5 is intended to give you some practice with pairing and simple acknowledgement responses. Try it now.

Worksheet 5

Linking

Student 1:
"That experience was fun. I liked having other students telling me what job they could see me doing in the future."

Student 2:
"I liked that part too. I also enjoyed the feedback from others in the class."

Your linking response:

Student 3:
"I would choose 'directing others' as my top job satisfier."

Student 4:
"I don't like the idea of directing or leading others. I'd rather have someone else take that responsibility."

Your linking response:

Student 5:
"If someone gave me a $1,000,000 dollars, I would invest it."

Student 6:
"Yeah, I'd put all of it in the bank."

Student 7:
"I'd put part of it in savings, but then I'd buy a new sports car."

Your linking response:

Simple Acknowledgement

Imagine that you are in the middle of a classroom discussion about Egypt. Something that was said has reminded Aaron of a recent unrelated family vacation experience and he begins to describe it to you. Your simple acknowledgement response:

Jason, a very outspoken student in your class, interrupts another student, John, who is responding to a question you posed regarding a local political event. Jason disagrees strongly with the other student's opinion and begins voicing his own ideas. Your response to Jason:

Sample responses to Worksheet 5 are found in the Appendix.

Chapter 5
Facilitative Feedback
Complimenting and Confronting

The previous sections focused on the facilitative teacher tuning into and responding to students. It is equally important, at appropriate times, to express your own thoughts, impressions, and feelings. You particularly want students to know where you stand in relation to their behaviors and ideas.

Students need feedback from you. They need to know how they are coming across to others. They want to know the kind of impact they are having. This includes the personal and academic aspects of their life. Students can benefit from feedback about themselves, their abilities, and their behaviors. But, like most of us, they dislike criticism. A facilitative teacher knows how to communicate both a compliment and a confrontation.

A key concept in any relationship is congruence—the ability to be authentic. Facilitative teachers are aware of their own experiences and what they are experiencing at the moment. This enables them to be more genuine and to relate their experience to students. Being genuine does not mean "telling it like it is," to the point of being insensitive or rude. Rather, it involves a form of communication in which people talk about the impact they are having on each other.

How can this be accomplished? Again, learning to be facilitative is not unlike learning to play golf—once you learn the club grip and how to swing the club, you still have to execute the skills in order to play the game. But golfers also know that the end result is only as great as the implementation of each skill of the game. By concentrating early on the small parts, they eventually become a totality—integrated, unified, and congruent.

The realities of teaching—overloaded classes, endless demands, sudden crises—make the job difficult. Teachers need not apologize for their frustration. Yet, effective teachers are aware of their feelings, pleasant and unpleasant, and accept responsibility for them. They want to be genuine and be facilitative. They search for the best words to communicate their thoughts and feelings and then present them in a way that is conducive to open communication.

Most teachers are in their jobs because they get something else from their work besides money. They experience the personal joy of learning with others, of seeing young people change in positive ways. These positive experiences are important to communicate to students and colleagues. Yet, many teachers report that giving compliments to others is just as awkward as confronting them. Expressing one's pleasant or unpleasant feelings is a skill, especially in facilitative teaching.

Facilitative teachers have mastered the art of giving feedback. They know how to express anger without insult, disappointment without guilt, and pride without embarrassment. Facilitative teachers describe what they see, what they feel, and what they expect. They focus on the situation (especially the behavior) and avoid attacking the person. "I am annoyed," "I am disappointed," "I am irritated" are more valid statements than, "You are a pest," "Now, look what you have done," "You are lazy," "Who do you think you are?"

When Mr. Hunt, a fourth grade teacher, was surprised at what he saw in his classroom one day he said, "I see some papers scattered over the floor. There are some chairs turned over and some of you are out of your assigned seats.... I'm surprised and... I'm concerned. We need to talk. Let's take time to talk about what's happening in here."Rather than rush in with a general reprimand of the class, this kind of feedback avoided insults and threats. Later, as it seemed timely, Mr. Hunt stressed some general procedures that would be followed when he was not in the classroom. In a sense, he carefully confronted his class.

In another situation, Ms. Darwin's fifth grade class was rambunctious. She consciously avoided attacking and threatening the students ("You're acting like a bunch of wild animals"). Instead, she gained their attention and stated firmly, "It's disappointing when I hear so much noise—like the slamming of desks and shouting across the room. It makes me think about being more strict with you, so I thought we had better explore this problem together." The noise subsided. The discussion continued to focus on the impact of their behavior on the teacher, and each other, and what might be done to make things better.

When Mrs. Brooks, a kindergarten teacher, saw five-year-old Alan throw a big piece of dirt at his friend, she said loudly, "I saw that, Alan. You threw dirt at James and now his shirt is messed up. I am really disappointed. We don't throw things at people, including dirt." The teacher intentionally tried to avoid insult and shame ("What's the matter with you? You could have hurt him. That was very mean and cruel.")

Two boys in the school cafeteria made "bullets" out of bread and threw them at each other and messed up the room. When the teacher discovered what happened, she sat the boys down across from one another and knelt down beside them. Then she said, "I really get frustrated when I see you throwing bread. It makes me want to say 'this has got to stop.' I'm disappointed and wondering now if you are going to need closer supervision." Without a word, the boys cleaned up the room. This teacher also avoided threats and insults ("Clean it up now... or else you're in big trouble! You're not living in a pig sty. Wait until your parents hear about this.")

During a cleanup period in kindergarten, a teacher was helping the children put away their play materials. Dora left her pile untouched and refused to help. "Dora, there are still some things to be put away," said the teacher. "I don't have to put them away if I don't want to," replied Dora. The teacher said firmly, "The rule is that blocks are to be put away during cleanup." The girl said defiantly, "You clean them up." The teacher smiled and said playfully, "Come on, I can pick up more than you can." This was not the best time for a confrontation and the teacher chose to lighten the situation by making a game of it.

Later, when Dora seemed more receptive, the teacher quietly pulled her aside and said, "Dora, I've been thinking about what happened this morning when you said you didn't want to pick up the blocks and that I should pick them up, even though I wasn't playing with them. That disappointed me and made we wonder what was happening that made you not want to put them away by yourself?" Dora tried to explain that another child, who had been playing with her shortly before cleanup time, had walked away to play with someone else and didn't return to help. This apparently made Dora angry and the thought of picking up the blocks by herself was annoying. The teacher responded to Dora's feelings and then clarified class rules and procedures. This was a timely confrontation where matters could be explored and feelings expressed. It was a situation in which learning could take place.

When teachers are upset, children usually become attentive. They are often worried because they aren't sure what teachers or adults will do with their negative feelings. As you know, teachers can be uncomfortable, displeased, annoyed, irritated, frustrated, exasperated, surprised, worried, confused, angry, disappointed, and discouraged. All teachers, including facilitative ones, experience unpleasant feelings at times. Learning how to express such feelings in a constructive way is not easy. Lost tempers can lead to regrettable remarks and conflict. Yet, effective communication between teacher and students depends on expressing unpleasant as well as pleasant feelings.

You can avoid words that humiliate—that denigrate a child's worth. Even when frustrated, you can find an appropriate way to vent the feeling. Self-imposed restraints are helpful but they need not lead to ignoring a situation or talking about it with bland expressions. To the contrary, they can enhance your teaching style.

Life in any school can be difficult. Many people struggle to be first in line. Some push themselves aggressively to the front. Others step aside, not knowing how to react. Children can learn to cope with this aspect of life when teachers and parents act as models. This includes showing children how to respond in a positive way when unpleasantness is present. As one teacher put it: "Even in anger, I say to myself: I may not be making any gains now, but I can minimize the losses! I've got to make sure that a rupture is not irreparable."

Feedback is letting people know the impact that their specific behavior is having on you—for better or for worse. It involves an honest reaction on your part. Feedback can be of different sorts. Many times teachers confront their students in an attempt to restore order. Sometimes the intent is to help a student examine the consequences of behavior. It should be an invitation to self-examination.

Facilitative feedback is a valuable part of a teacher's skills. Here are three helpful guidelines:

1. **Be specific about the behavior. Give examples.**
2. **Tell how the behavior makes you feel when it occurs. This is the impact that the behavior has on you.**
3. **Tell what your feelings make you want to do.**

These three simple parts can help you give constructive feedback. They are especially effective when giving a compliment or a gentle confrontation. When a personal conflict reaches a crisis stage, communication between individuals is difficult and strained because each is defensive. Don't wait to give feedback until a crisis occurs.

When giving students feedback, avoid advice, judging, or labeling. Give attention to those things that a student can change. It's not helpful to focus on things about which the person can do nothing (e.g. race, gender, physical handicap, and so forth).

Telling a class that they have "been very good" is not specific enough. If you return from the principal's office and the students are working in their seats, you might begin by saying, "When I walked in the room and saw that each of you was working quietly on your assignments...." This immediately directs their attention to some behavior.

In another case you could say: "John, you keep leaving your desk to sharpen your pencil while I'm talking to the rest of the class, even though I asked you not to. You just stood up and walked across the room when we were having a class discussion...." The next step is to tell Johnny how this particular behavior of his makes you feel.

What do you experience when you see John being disruptive? "...I felt myself getting upset and even angry." Now tell him what your feelings make you want to do in this situation. How do your feelings in this case affect how you act or want to act. "Those feelings make me want to say to you, that if it happens again, you will have to stay in the room at lunch time and we will have a longer talk about the matter."

When confronting someone, watch your choice of words. Avoid expressions which are too intense and which tend to bring about defensiveness. Try to build a positive relationship before confronting students. Do this by using some other facilitative responses (e.g.

93

feeling-focused responses). This will give you some "chips in the bank" and they can be drawn upon as you need them. Confronting affects the relationship. It inevitably "draws a chip from the bank and cashes it in," hopefully to improve the relationship. Facilitative teachers make it a point to build a reserve so that a confrontation will have some power and the relationship will not go bankrupt.

Learning theory tells us that it is better to focus upon what you like, or to reinforce the positive. Learning theory also suggests that we should give more attention, compliments, and rewards when behavior is appropriate and try to ignore inappropriate behavior. Therefore, you will want to look for more opportunity to give positive feedback and be cautious when confronting.

Finally, you can mix the parts (guidelines) when formulating a feedback response. That is, you can first begin with your feeling, then move to what the feeling makes you want to do, and then to the behavior that seem to stimulate the feeling. Or, you can start by telling what you want to do because of a feeling and how that feeling came about. The parts are only a formula around which you can communicate your thoughts and feelings.

Worksheet 6 provides you the opportunity to practice feedback responses. Please complete it now.

Worksheet 6

In the following activity, write your feedback message to each of the stimulus situations. Keep the three parts in mind.

1. You are busy with the morning lunch count. A group of students have gathered at one of the activity centers and are busy visiting quietly and completing activities. When you finish and gather the class together, you say...

2. You send a small group of students to the library to work on their own. You notice them walking together quietly on their way back to your class. When they walk into the room, you say....

3. A visitor comes to your classroom. You must stop your work with a small group of students to talk with this person. The group continues quietly with their work until you return. Your response....

4. In physical education, a few students refuse to take part in the activities. What's worse, they interrupt the games of others by shouting at them, and making teasing remarks. You say....

5. Some students have been working on a papier-mache project in the art center. Suddenly, in fun, one child begins flinging the sticky paper at the other children. Squeals of laughter bring you over to find the center and children are covered with messy paper and paste. Your response....

Sample responses to Worksheet 6 are found in the Appendix.

Chapter 6

Facilitative Discipline, Problem-solving, and Classroom Management

Good Teaching is Good Discipline and Guidance

Almost everyone, including teachers, parents, administrators, and even students, is concerned about school discipline. It continues to be the number one concern of educators (Phi Delta Kappan polls) and of parents (Gallup polls) over the past few decades. They want schools that have good discipline. But, what does that mean?

What is Discipline?

For many people, discipline is equated with control. More specifically, it is the control of students and their management. A school or classroom in which there is good discipline is typically viewed as an orderly place where students do what is expected of them. It implies that there is a rather quiet and studious atmosphere where students cooperatively follow a code of conduct. Teachers give directions and students follow them.

When the word discipline is mentioned to some people, they immediately think of punishment. It is the consequence for the non-compliant. If rules are disobeyed or procedures are not followed, discipline is administered by authority figures. Punitive measures, such as paddlings (corporal punishment), suspensions or detentions, verbal reprimands, or a denial of privileges are often listed as a means of disciplining students. It is assumed that students with "bad attitudes" need to be confronted with strict and sometimes harsh consequences in order to teach them a lesson.

Some enlightened people describe discipline as a means of self-control, where an individual trains oneself to perform in certain ways. Do you have any self-discipline when it comes to meeting a challenge (a regular exercise program) or denying yourself something (turning down a high calorie dessert)? Self-discipline involves character and skill development. A disciplined person knows how to approach matters in a systematic way and can stay focused on a task.

Discipline can also refer to a branch of learning or an area of knowledge, such as the discipline of mathematics. The study of school and classroom discipline is a discipline that all teachers should pursue.

To the majority of people, educators are in charge of a no-nonsense system in which students follow rules. Rules are fairly but strictly enforced. Thus, students learn in a logical, structured, and orderly environment. When a student is out of order or misbehaves, then there is a discipline problem which needs attention. The goal of teachers, of course, is to have a preventive program in which discipline cases are the exception rather than the rule.

What Makes Students Misbehave?

There are many explanations which account for student behavior. Some theories attempt to identify the underlying causes of misbehavior: wanting attention, feeling bored, seeking revenge, believing that one is a failure, fearing rejection, having to prove something, lacking impulse control, suffering from biochemical or neurological disorders, needing social skills, having inappropriate habits. And, the list can go on. Probably all of these reasons have some degree of truth to them when we examine discipline cases.

While theories of misbehavior may be interesting and, on occasion, give us clues in a particular case, they are often confusing and often fail to give us direction. Many of the theoretical principles are misunderstood, misinterpreted, or chosen piecemeal in order to confirm a disciplinary action or stance. In general, too much attention is already given to analyzing causes rather than attending to feasible skills and actions which are needed to improve the learning environment. In addition, most educators lack an understanding of their own goals, interests, needs, and values, in order to embrace or develop a complete theory of misbehavior and discipline.

It is not our intent to present the work of others or a lengthy discussion of various models and theories about student behavior and misbehavior. You can find other resources and become familiar with the range of theories. Study in depth those which appeal to you. Our own experience is that there is neither a single nor a right theory that works best in every situation or which can be uniformily applied to everyone. Rather, it is the integration of theoretical knowledge with one's personal attitude and interpersonal skills which determine how conflict is prevented or resolved. Conflict is the critical factor which must be addressed in every discipline situation.

Conflict results from individuals who, earnestly seeking to meet their needs and interests, are confronted with limits. Some limits result from the working or social parameters which are imposed on them by authority figures. Other limits are a consequence of powerful cultural or peer influences. Of course, it is also possible to have conflict when there are no limits, no rules, and anything goes. In a sense, conflict is an inevitable part of all group relationships, since there are so many needs and interests represented. Therefore, control is the central issue—external control and self-control.

The facilitative model enables a teacher to first explore a situation, perhaps by getting students to talk about their lives and situations. The conflict may be a consequence of encountering a school or classroom rule and being confronted by adults or other students. As a facilitator, you could attempt to present options and choices, examine consequences and alternatives. You could emphasize the development of social skills and cognitive awareness of social mores and customs, preferably before an incident requires immediate action. Although we can learn from a crisis and, with facilitative skills, work our way out of it, it is easier when skills are developed and used to resolve a conflict before it becomes an intense and critical event.

Preventing Discipline Problems

The prevention of discipline problems, whether they be in school or in a classroom, is directly related to interpersonal relationships and skills. Conflicts can be reduced and managed, if not eliminated, by first developing appropriate social skills among students and teachers. This, in turn, enables people to foster the helping or facilitative conditions (e.g. respect, trust, understanding, and so forth), which leads to positive interpersonal relationships. These relationships form the foundation on which to avoid stress and dissension, as well as to process a problem when it develops. Teaching students the facilitative model might be a starting place in a preventive approach.

After students, and teachers, have attained interpersonal skills and practice in developing positive relationships, appropriate school roles and procedures for students and teachers can be outlined and discussed. There can be no mistake that teachers and administrators are charged by school boards and the public to present and implement a curriculum in a disciplined climate. Certain student outcomes are expected. Desired student behaviors are expected, with consequences for acceptable and unacceptable behaviors defined. Moreover, expected teacher behaviors can also be recognized and are subject to being reviewed and discussed by teachers and students. Discipline is a two-way street, where all participants in the learning process are expected to follow a reasonable set of guidelines which respect individual and group rights.

Classroom Discipline

Facilitative teachers begin by developing a list of classroom guidelines or rules for students. The rules are related to helping students help each other to learn. They are stated in the positive. As a whole they can be considered a social contract, one which is clear, precise, and negotiable. As additional rules are needed, students and teacher talk about them before they are added. Some required guidelines or rules might be eliminated, especially as students and teachers learn to work cooperatively together.

Rule making can be a powerful learning experience for you and your students. Try not to have too many rules. A long and detailed list of rules and procedures can set you up as a full-time enforcer. Some students are bound to test the limits and a lengthy list provides more opportunities for conflict and a challenge of authority.

Classroom or school rules that are vague (e.g. "Respect the rights of others." "Be a responsible person." "Have a good attitude.") almost always lead to conflict. Those stated in the negative (e.g. "Don't be late." "No talking during independent study times." "No running in the hallways.") emphasize obedience rather than achievement. If these same rules were worded positively and precisely (e.g. "Be to class on time." "Study quietly." "Slow down and walk in the hallways.") they would tell students what to do rather than what not to do. Describing the behavior that is expected implants a cognitive thought that can be used to guide a person's actions.

Once a set of rules and procedures have been agreed upon, students are encouraged to talk about their experiences, their feelings, and possible alternatives. Student awareness of expectations, their experiences, and knowledge of roles are important in preventing discipline problems. Likewise, for teachers there should be an awareness of their own expectations, roles, and the rules and procedures under which they work. There is a need for both students and teachers to be aware of the circumstances which tend to influence their decisions.

Teachers have needs and feelings too. They cannot be ignored. Being aware of them is an essential component of managing students and having and maintaining good discipline. Too many teachers suffer from excessive stress, severe headaches, sleepless nights, and depression because they dread working with difficult students. They are unsure what to do, fearing their authority will be challenged and that a perceived weakness on their part will lead to more problems. Insecure and unskilled teachers tend to rush in with outdated rules, threats, demands, and ill-chosen words when they are experiencing unpleasant feelings.

Even the most caring and understanding teachers can become irritated, annoyed, angry, or discouraged with troublesome students. They have days when their energy level is low and they are less responsive, thus making them vulnerable to saying and doing things that are less than facilitative. However, facilitative teachers are more aware of their feelings and the impact of their actions on students. They not only tolerate feedback from students, they elicit it and value it. They are not afraid of making mistakes, of being open and honest with students about what they are experiencing.

It cannot be denied that teachers have different personalities, different styles of working with people, and different expectations. Some teachers work with few rules, while others work best in a tightly structured environment. As long as students like school, are achieving, and working well with teachers and their classmates, then these differences are insignificant. As each teacher establishes a positive working relationship with students, there is also less need for school-wide rules and polices that attempt to affect all classrooms and faculty. School-wide policies, while valuable in their own right, can take away the prerogative of some teachers and their students and should be limited.

Facilitative Teachers Give Feedback and Set Limits

We have already presented the facilitative feedback model, which consists of being specific about the behavior that you have noticed, telling what you are experiencing (feeling), and what you are inclined to do. The third part is not necessarily an annoucement of an action that you will take, or a punitive measure that will be implemented. Rather, it focuses on the considered thoughts and behaviors which come to mind when you feel certain ways. These feelings, of course, are tied closely to your perceptions of the person's behavior.

The best time to give feedback to troublesome students is after you have talked quietly with them about a situation (building up some "chips in the bank") and tried to reach more knowledge and understanding. In the process a student is encouraged to think more about one's behavior, the impact that it has on others, and alternatives. Sometimes private discussions lead to further clarification of rules and procedures. When done privately, an individual has an opportunity to "save face" and not be embarrassed and defensive in front of classmates. While an individual meeting about a conflict is the preferred mode, because it is easier to manage and control, there will be times when a group discussion cannot be avoided and may be the best choice.

Suppose that you are being interrupted while talking with someone. You may need to turn to the intruder and "set a limit." You might say, for instance, "I'm aware that it's not easy for you to wait, and whatever you have to say is very important to you; *however*, I can't give my attention to you now. When I have finished here, I will talk with you." Attention then is directed back to the original task.

In this case, you are acknowledging the feelings and request, but you do not engage the student in a conversation or immediately honor the request. With demanding students, it is possible that a similar message may have to be repeated, but again the person is told to wait.

Likewise, a group of students may be carrying on private aside conversations which distract from a class discussion. You may say, "Hold it a minute. We have too many people talking at once and the private talks that some of you are having is making things confusing. What you have to say is interesting, maybe more interesting than what we are doing, but we need your attention now." Then, without engaging in criticism or argument, you could redirect everyone back to the task at hand.

One student told his classroom teacher that she had a stupid rule and that other teachers didn't have such a rule. The teacher replied, "You don't understand why we have such a rule and it makes no sense to you. You could work just as well without it. Nevertheless, it's a rule that I'm comfortable with and want to keep. Therefore, you will have to go along with it."

In this instance, there is no argument, no attempt to explain or develop a rationale for the rule. At least not at this time. It may, in fact, be a silly and unnecessary rule by some standards. The rule makes no difference as long as the teacher knows that some students will have problems with it and experience unpleasant feelings. They can learn to deal with those feelings in a socially appropriate way, acknowledging that the teacher is doing the best that one can in that role. While facilitative teachers have fewer rules, and fewer conflicts, they can establish special procedures that might be considered by others as peculiar or idiosyncratic. Their working relationship with students enables them to "cash in a few chips" on occasion and to get students to go along with them.

Working With Troubled Students

We heard it before, "Times have changed and young people are different. We are dealing with a new set of problems which affect our schools." Actually, while many of the old problems remain, new ones have been added or intensified. The following lists compare discipline problems and concerns in the 1940s to the 1980s (1988):

1940s	1980s
Talking	Drug abuse
Chewing gum	Alcohol abuse
Making noise	Suicide
Running in the hallways	Pregnancy
Getting out of place in line	Rape
Wearing improper clothing	Robbery
Not putting paper in wastebaskets	Assault
	Burglary
	Arson
	Bombings

Contemporary youth have more choices and face more problems in their neighborhoods and their schools. Some of the same issues over classroom behavior and school discipline have remained constant over the decades (e.g. Inappropriate talking, fighting, dress codes). The second list emphasizes misconduct that is not only more serious but even criminal.

There are many students who are required to attend school who do not want to be there. They are potential dropouts or pushouts. They tend to see themselves as failures and, as part of their psychological defenses, they take on a don't care attitude or adopt a tough guy ("You can't hurt me, but I can hurt you") image. It is not easy to work with students who have negative attitudes, who defy you to show them that learning can be fun, imaginative, and relevant.

Close to a million school-aged youths annually drop out of school. Yet, one study in 1983 indicated that over 50% of the dropouts had no record of disciplinary infractions and only 17% were failing classes. In more than 40% of the cases, the reason given for leaving school was because of poor teacher-student relationships. When talking about teachers the dropouts used such expressions as, "They put you down," "They don't care about me," "They give you a hard time."

Convinced that there are no adults in their schools to whom they could turn to, to talk with, 72% of the dropouts in one national survey reported that they did not consult with any school personnel before leaving school. And, more than 70% said that they would have stayed in school if teacher-student relationships had been different...."If we were treated as students not as inmates," and "If teachers weren't so boring... if it (school) was more interesting."

Teachers as Student Advisors

One of the most innovative approaches to school discipline and to building positive school climates, is the teachers as advisors program (TAP). It was first introduced in the middle schools, as part of a homeroom or homebase period, and was probably an extension of classroom guidance in elementary schools. It is now being advocated for all grade levels.

When the first books were written about guidance and counseling, all of them were directed to the work of classroom teachers. There were few, if any, specialists such as counselors, school psychologists or social workers. For a period of time it was assumed that specialists should be responsible for working with difficult students and making them better learners. Now, it is clear that good guidance is good teaching. Good teaching is good discipline. Good discipline is part of a good guidance program which involves all personnel in a school.

It is assumed that every student needs a friendly adult in school who knows and cares about the student in a personal way. Something must be done to show caring, understanding, and respect. In general, teachers in TAP are assigned about 20 advisees each. They meet their advisees on a regular basis, usually as a group every day for about 25-30 minutes. At least twice a week, teachers involve their advisees in group guidance lessons and activities. It is also a time to build positive relationships, to form a support group of peers, and to explore personal interests, goals, and concerns. It is also in TAP that conflict situations and related issues which appear to get in the way of effective academic learning are addressed.

The two-day a week guidance lessons are typically built around a guidance curriculum and guidance units which encourage students to be more responsible for themselves and take an active part in developing positive working relationships with their peers and teachers. For example, here is a list of the 12 units that were included in one middle school.

> Getting Acquainted—Orientation to School
> Study Skills and Habits—Time Management
> Self-assessment
> Communications Skills
> Decision-making and Problem-solving
> Peer Relationships
> Motivation
> Conflict/Resolution
> Wellness—Common Health Issues
> Career Development
> Educational Planning
> Community Pride and Involvement

Each of these units consisted of about five or six 30-minute sessions presented during TAP periods, which enabled teacher-advisors to complete a unit in about three weeks. The other three days for TAP, which take place at the same time during the week, were given to individual conferences as most students used the time for quiet study, silent reading or writing, and tutoring sessions.

TAP has been described in more detail elsewhere (Myrick, 1988), as part of a school-wide developmental guidance program. The basic principles of developmental guidance are:

It is for all students
It has an organized and planned curriculum (e.g. TAP)
It is sequential and flexible
It is an integrated part of the total educational process
It involves all school personnel
It helps students learn more effectively and efficiently
It includes school counselors, as personnel, who provide specialized counseling services.

Teachers are the key to developmental guidance and, subsequently, they help prevent discipline problems in school and in classrooms. However, without preparation in interpersonal skills, the facilitative model, and ways to lead group guidance discussions, most teachers will struggle and may be less successful than they would otherwise be. With training, materials and suggested activities, enough time, and administrative support, TAP can make schools a better place to be for everybody.

Clearly, the other key to discipline is responsible self-control, which both students and teachers can obtain. It should not be taken for granted, as the skills and attitudes that make such control possible must be learned and practiced. Students who are continual behavior problems and who are non-compliant are a genuine concern. Some of these students will need to be referred to specialists, who have more training than teachers in working with dysfunctional people. Yet, eventually these same students are sent back to their classroom teachers, who have more direct contact with them than most specialists and parents.

The key to reaching the most difficult students is to build positive relationships with them in advance of critical moments. Many of these students are so dysfunctioning that they lack self-control and inevitably get out of line. They should be targeted for early intervention, for special attention in TAP, and for help by specialists. Let them know that you care and are interested in them, but be prepared for rejection. If they are receptive, it means that they are giving you the benefit of the doubt and not generalizing from their previous unhappy experiences. Take advantage of it by focusing on the positive with them.

One of the authors was given a list of do's and don'ts for effective discipline. It was assumed that the list provided a thoughtful set of guidelines for teachers. The list, in general, is as follows:

1. Be realistic in your expectations of your students' behavior and/or skill development. Give them time to adapt to new situations and procedures.

2. Be friendly, but firm with all students, both in and out of the classroom. Make your presence felt in a positive way.

3. Avoid sarcasm. Be sensitive when choosing your words.

4. Be yourself. You will not gain favor with students by trying to be one of them. They want you to be their friendly teacher not their best buddy.

5. Remember that you were once a young student. Think about those teachers who you thought were respectful and helpful, when trying to resolve a conflict. Ask yourself: "Would you like to be a student in your class?"

6. When conflict arises, take some time to think.... Count to ten, if it helps. You might develop a personal signal or cue that relaxes and calms you. If you're uncertain, it's probably better to do nothing at the moment, especially if you are angry.

7. Begin and end your class on time. Having a routine helps. Students benefit from consistent structure.

8. Start each class with a smile and enthusiasm. Smile more.

9. Once a difficult case has been resolved, follow-up with a some kind of positive interaction. There is no need to hold a grudge or be unforgiving.

10. Avoid setting a rule you can't or don't want to enforce.

11. Use a warm sense of humor when you can... perhaps "kid" a student out of disruptive behavior. Being light-hearted at times can ease the pressure in a stressful situation. However, be sensitive to the moment.

12. Designate a special "time out" area in your room, or identify a place where students can go when they need time out from the class and the class needs time out from them.

13. Ignore disruptive behavior where possible, using a few subtle cues to bring a student or group back on task. Making an issue of every inappropriate behavior can be a tedious and self-defeating job. There are, of course, some misbehaviors that need immediate attention.

14. Share your classroom rules with other teachers and administrators, openly asking for their feelings and ideas. Use the information to refine your list and to improve your interactions with students. Remember that a rule on someone else's list may not fit your style and need not be automatically included.

15. Avoid the witholding of special area classes (art, physical education, music) as punishment for inappropriate behavior.

16. If a problem persists, communicate your concern with others and begin, if you have not done so already, constructing a case which describes what you have already done, time, places, and outcomes. If the problem still persists, talk with the school counselor or perhaps another teacher. If the problem continues to persist, talk again with the counselor and administrator, who might involve other specialists. Talk with the parents. If the problem still persists after several efforts, construct your case again on paper and refer the student and ask for special assistance.

17. Avoid threatening or punishing a group for what an individual has done.

18. Identify leaders in the class who can become your models for others. Give attention to a student who is performing as expected so that others can hear you.

19. Learn and use the names of students as you talk and work with them.

20. Call upon those students whose attention is wavering, but not in an embarrassing manner.

21. Study the seating arrangements of your students. Ask yourself what might be done to make things work better. Divide the class into different kinds of working groups on occasion rather than staying in one fixed position all the time.

22. Personal appearance, tone of voice, and attitude affect student behavior. Little idiosyncrasies and mannerisms can detract from your effectiveness. Take inventory of yourself and ask students for feedback.

23. Develop a feeling of togetherness and group cohesiveness in your class... a "we" feeling.

24. Encourage your students to "tune into the feelings" of other students and/or ask them to "clarify" what another student just said. The more facilitators in your classroom the better!

25. Work on building a positive relationship through facilitative responses, especially with those who seem more troubled than others. Get your students involved in the learning process through personalized activities.

Problem-solving

Problem-solving methods in day-to-day human relations may be the most essential skill we can teach students. It is essential to academic study and a critical element in interpersonal relationships. In the art of problem-solving, teachers pose hypothetical problems to students in an attempt to help them use their minds, to think through a situation, to apply what they have been learning. Teachers can also use problem-solving techniques to help students think about personal matters and the decisions that they are trying to make.

For example, a teacher of chemistry might set up a problem where students work together to identify the components of a lab experiment. An English teacher could ask students to write business letters to a company in order to request warranty service. A social studies teacher may ask students how they would plan for a journey to a distant planet, knowing that they could only take ten things with them.

In other situations, the teacher may be asked to speak to students about their attitudes or conduct in class, or perhaps the way in which they are approaching class assignments. A group of students might request assistance with a problem which involves other students or teachers. In these cases, the teacher also applies and models problem-solving strategies or techniques.

Problem-solving has been advanced as outstanding teaching methodology when helping young people learn math, science, social studies, or a language. But, only a few teachers seem able to facilitate learning when a social or personal problem develops. Using your facilitative skills, you can help students solve all kinds of problems.

Facilitative teachers recognize that effective problem-solving is a skill that students can and need to learn and practice. In addition, facilitative teachers know that they can model problem-solving behaviors. As students watch teachers solve problems, especially interpersonal ones, they learn how to apply what they have learned in their academic lessons. One's ability to help solve a problem, of course, is related to a knowledge of the problem-solving process.

Problem-solving creates anxious moments. Some problems are more stressful and frustrating than others. Some require immediate attention and must be addressed quickly. Crises cannot always be avoided, even when the best available plan is being followed. Other problems are less complex and can be broken down easier into easily-identified successive steps.

A review of the professional literature suggests that problem-solving and decision-making usually involve several steps. First, *identify the problem*. What is happening that is creating the problem? Who is involved and what roles are they playing? This is often a difficult task, as the presenting problem may not be the "real" problem. The presenting or current problem may only be a symptom. Or, it may only be a safe place in which to begin to explore ideas.

Second, *define the problem*. As you continue to explore the problem with someone, you will want to help them break the problem down so that it can be better understood and managed. Defining the problem in specific terms and behaviors is useful. It also leads to general and specific goals.

Third, after a person has a better understanding of what is to be accomplished or resolved, *the alternative courses of action can be examined*. This may involve an exploration of values, as well as some possible next steps. Some people have found it helpful to build a "value hierarchy" in an attempt to identify the values that influence decision-making. Ideas might be listed and then given a positive or negative weighting in terms of their significance. The values might be ranked from most to least important and related to the alternatives. Consequences are considered.

Finally, *select a course of action,* develop the idea and then act upon it. Obviously, this involves some choices. For example, suppose that you have in your classroom a student who is disturbing the study of others by interrupting them with silly, disparaging remarks. After some initial laughter, students in the class are now beginning to show signs of being irritated by the person's remarks and they are looking for you to do something. You have some choices. You could threaten action, if it continues. You can reprimand. You could excuse the student from the class, or perhaps you could administer some form of punishment, such as giving a failing grade in citizenship or denying the person some classroom privileges. Or, you could hold a class discussion and discuss classroom behavior. Students might be given an opportunity to solve the problem, through some systematic steps. The student's behavior is just as much the class' problem as it is yours. But, these are all alternatives, and there are more. What will you choose?

Our choices are influenced by values, but they are also affected by our habits and skills. If you have slipped into some convenient habits of problem-solving that are effective, then you will continue to use them. Identify and assess your skills and habits. Do they help you to be as effective as you would like to be? Do they match well with what you value and the limits within which you work as a teacher?

Problem-solving is a skill that can be developed. Being organized and having some sense of direction can be comforting as well as practical. One systematic approach to problem-solving that has been used by many facilitative teachers emphasizes that you place responsibility on the students. It leads them through a thinking process and, in this respect, teaches them a strategy that can be used when they encounter other problems. While it encourages them to assume responsibility, explore, and make the decisions, it also gives you room to offer timely suggestions or advice. Let's examine this problem-solving model in more detail.

The problem-solving model consists of four basic stages, each characterized by an open-ended question which helps focus the discussion on the problem. Moreover, these questions, or steps, are put in a sequential order that helps structure the flow of conversation and the thinking process. In general, the four key questions have a tendency to fall naturally in most discussions.

A Problem-solving Model

"What is the problem or situation?" Begin by asking this open-ended question which allows the student or students to tell you what they are thinking and feeling. Be alert to opportunities to show your understanding and respect by responding with some high facilitative responses. It is especially important to respond to feelings as students share their perspectives. At this point, you are helping them to identify the problem and to demonstrate that you are interested in further exploring the matter with them.

"What have you tried?" After a student's initial attempt to describe the situation, this question focuses attention to any action that has already been taken. There is no use in making a suggestion that someone has already tried. Or, if something has been tried which seems like a reasonable solution, you might follow this basic question with another: "And, how did that work out?" Or, "Okay, and how did you go about doing that?" These follow-up questions will provide an opportunity to discover if what was tried seemed workable and if it might be tried again with a few changes. This key question often catches some people off-guard. For example, asking a young person what has been done to resolve a problem with a teacher can be thought provoking, as many students choose only to complain rather than take some positive action.

"What else could you do?" This question is designed to encourage people to think more about their situations and to consider some possible courses of actions or alternatives that might be tried. As they think about the matter, ideas might come to mind that they haven't considered, perhaps because they haven't had an opportunity to think about it in a systematic way. Such a question also puts more responsibility on them and sets the stage for you to give some timely advice or ideas, if you have any. After hearing what might be done, you can add your suggestions to the list. You might also pose the questions, "How would you go about doing that?" or, "How do you think that might turn out?" Again, exploring possible alternatives and consequences will require the use of the high facilitative responses.

"What is your next step?" Finally, after considering possible courses of action and their consequences, it is time to help the person take some action. It is not enough for most people to simply think about a problem. Some hope that it will go away, as they are contemplating about it. Others are so unsure of what they want to have happen or what they want to do that they feel paralyzed and end up taking no action at all. Still others realize that implementing a course of action, taking a "next step," is what decision-making is about. It is even possible that the next step might be to wait for a period of time before doing anything. Even this would be part of a planned approach and considered a relevant solution for the time being.

These four problem-solving steps, or key questions, can be used with an individual or a group. Students may come to you with a problem or you may decide to bring a problem to their attention. For instance, suppose that a young girl is having problems completing her English assignments. You may decide it is time to confront her and say something like this: "It seems, Elizabeth, that you have a problem when it comes to your English assignments. What's the situation?" And, then the other questions are asked in sequence as the matter is discussed. This approach coaches Elizabeth in a thinking process and could perhaps help her resolve a problem of which she is unaware or is denying or ignoring.

A class might be willing to discuss a problem that the student body in the school is considering. A class discussion could follow along the same problem-solving steps. Likewise, a small group of students might tell you about a problem that they are having with a particular student who is bothersome to them. As you listen to them speak about their concerns, you could draw upon the problem-solving model to help them take some responsible action. Finally, this problem-solving model might be practiced in an academic lesson, such as an international problem that is being studied in social studies, or a problem confronting a person in literature. It can be especially helpful in approaching problems in science or math.

The facilitative teacher models problem-solving approaches and uses facilitative responses to help students think about difficult situations. Responsible decision-making comes from practice and having opportunities to be a problem solver.

Managing Classroom Groups

Classroom management has been used to describe how teachers interact with students and move them toward cooperative classroom behaviors. In our way of thinking it focuses on the physical movement of students, materials, and equipment. All of these, of course, have an impact on the learning atmosphere because they affect they dynamics of the group.

Effective classroom management, the actual physical arrangement of students in a classroom, can stimulate class interest, problem-solving, and play an important part in preventing discipline problems. When students cannot hear or see, they become disinterested and bored. Some silently withdraw while others become disruptive. These students are uninvolved in whatever lesson might be taking place and are unlikely to participate in your class activities.

When classes are physically arranged so that student involvement is high, then increased student participation can be expected. Let's look at some possible classroom arrangements and their impact upon students.

The Line-ups

First, there is the traditional "line them up in rows" approach. For instance, you might have 25 students in class who are arranged in five rows across the front, with five students each. It is the most commonly viewed classroom arrangement in all schools at all grade levels.

Seating students in lines and rows is frequently used because of tradition and because no other arrangement gives more attention to the person who is in front of the class. That is, all eyes are upon the teacher. The teacher is in control and discussion is almost always routed through the teacher. Yet, this arrangement is the least likely to encourage class discussion. Eye contact with others is limited and it is difficult to know the kind of impact that one's contribution is having upon others, unless you are the teacher. Therefore, if your primary goal is to impart information with limited discussion, then this is probably the best arrangement of chairs and students.

If you use this arrangement because it is convenient or because other arrangements of desks are infeasible or too cumbersome, recognize the limitations and think of ways in which you can group your students by physically moving yourself to a section of the room. For instance, you may at times call upon one line or one row. Or, in your mind you might divide the class configuration into quadrants. Then, using gestures or pointing out the imaginary boundaries, call upon one group of students sitting in a particular section to participate for a short time, as the others observe. You can also use this technique to scan the room, to elicit questions, or to direct your eyes as you make a presentation.

Semi-circles

Some teachers, recognizing the limitations of having students in rows when it comes to class discussion, arrange chairs in a large semi-circle. Or, they might use more than one semi-circle, one behind the other, if there is a large number of students and space is limited. This is a compromise. It focuses attention to the front of the room, yet increases eye contact among students. Although still limited, students tend to experience each other more as part of a group.

The semi-circle might appear to some as a horseshoe shaped arrangement. However, semi-circles can also be used when the class is divided into five or six smaller groups. These groups, sitting in a semi-circles can be arranged almost anywhere in the room, as long as the open part of the circle is directed to the teacher's podium or station.

Circles

If the classroom is large enough and the number of students is reasonable, a circle arrangement might prove valuable. This enables the teacher to gain control of the class through eye contact with all but a few who are seated to the immediate left and right of wherever the teacher might stand or sit. But, it also provides more opportunity for students to stimulate and respond to each other when discussion takes place. They can see one another and there is no one to hide behind. Consequently, there is a feeling of openness and togetherness which is not sensed in other arrangements.

The larger the group, the more limited the circle arrangement. In order to obtain a circle and, yet, seat everyone comfortably, the distance across the circle becomes impractical with a large group (over 30). There is a tendency for people to shout rather than talk comfortably. Side conversations are a natural consequence when the circle is too large. In addition, few classrooms can accommodate a large circle and too many times the arrangement looks like a rectangle. While this might prove interesting at times, the result is four rows, with two across from each other. Eye contact down the row is almost as difficult as it is in traditional rows. Nevertheless, circles promote more of a feeling of togetherness and group participation than do traditional lines.

Inside-outside Circles

One variation of circles is to have a large circle of students on the outside and a smaller group on the inside. This inside-outside group arrangement is especially useful when you are trying to demonstrate something. The inside group members are your helpers or active participants, while the outside group members observe. Giving the outside group a task—something to look for or to take note of—will help them stay more involved.

This approach has sometimes been called the "fishbowl" technique. The small group of students inside may feel like they are on stage, on the spot, or being scrutinized. For some students, this will produce a self-conscious feeling and they may feel embarrassed or shy. Yet, with practice the inside group learns to shut the outside group out of their mind. Consequently, the inside group members may have to be encouraged to speak up so that those on the outside can hear. However, that is not easy. Therefore, as a facilitator you may need to ask inside group members to speak louder, to repeat something, or perhaps to emphasize what was said through a clarification.

Generally, student participation from the outer circle is limited, although some activities have provisions for students to come forward and sit in an empty chair if they have something to say. After one group of students has been in the inner circle and completed a task, another group switches places with them and similar tasks or procedures continue. This procedure encourages listening and sharing ideas. Everyone gets an opportunity and the arrangement communicates expectations—listening or talking.

The Classroom Management Model

One rather innovative discussion technique uses a combination of approaches and is especially helpful when teachers have large numbers of students. It is called simply "the classroom management model" (Myrick, 1988) and capitalizes on the group dynamics that it generates. Here is how it works.

First, students are organized into discussion teams. No more than five teams are preferred. Although this technique has been proven valuable with very large groups, (e.g. over 100) discussion becomes more difficult to manage and involved if the number of teams exceeds six. It is best if the groups have equal numbers of students so that teams finish an assigned classroom activity about the same time.

Next, students are positioned around the room in semi-circles, each facing the front of the room. Thus, five semi-circled teams might be placed in such a way as to occupy each of the four corners and the middle of the classroom. Because the teams are facing the teacher, who is in the front of the room, discussion can take place by group or team and directed by the teacher. For example, a teacher might ask questions of a team, rather than individuals on that team. This gets the attention of the team members rather than one person. Students combine their efforts to answer a question or complete a task. Excitement usually runs high with this approach as students are more alert. Peer influence and pressure is also present.

Then, usually for a second activity, teams are asked to sit in circles. For instance, one student on the end of a semi-circled team might be responsible for moving to close the circle. This closed group can then be given a "go around" task in which each person is asked to respond. More than one task might be given to the teams in their closed group arrangement and after everyone has had an opportunity to talk, students are encouraged to ask questions of their team members. The teacher, naturally, moves around the room and helps keep the teams on task, answers questions briefly, or steps in with some timely teaching on occasion.

Finally, the teams are repositioned in their semi-circles, which is more conducive to a whole class discussion. Discussion may proceed by teams or with individuals who are seated with their teams.

A series of class activities around a theme or topic can take place in this model. Without exception, student interest, participation, and involvement with the lesson tend to run higher. This approach generates enthusiasm and gives everyone an opportunity to participate more often, in contrast to the traditional approach of leading a discussion while students are seated in rows.

Dyads and Triads

In addition to these arrangements, students can learn to work in triads and dyads. Although the noise level will increase, students quickly adjust and they learn to shut out external distractions. The success of these small groups often depends upon the task that is given, the time that is allowed, the experience that students have in working within small groups, and the supervision of teachers who move about their rooms encouraging and motivating the groups.

Dyads, or pairing students, is used when the teacher wants to have all students participate in a short period of time. Each member of the dyad usually takes turns doing a task, while the other facilitates. In triads a third member is added. This person might be an observer, or a second facilitator. In some case, all three are given the same task, perhaps a general discussion topic. Obviously, a group of three provides more opportunity for class members to talk and be heard than in a group of six or more.

After dyads or triads have been working for awhile, it is possible to combine some of them to form larger groups, perhaps a group of six. Groups of six have proven time after time to be the optimal small group size for sharing and exploring ideas. Go arounds, where one person starts and the person on the left then follows with the next comment, is a viable procedure which ensures that all group members will have a chance to respond and that an orderly procedure will be followed which keeps groups on task.

Facilitative teachers know about group dynamics and how to use them to their advantage. They know which activities might best be approached in small groups within the classroom and which ones lend themselves to a whole-class discussion. They deliberately mix students in different groups. They are aware that as students come to know each other better through small and large group activities, they feel better understood and accepted. Their contributions appear to be valued and, subsequently, they help create a more positive classroom environment for themselves and others.

Do you use the same physical arrangement of students day after day? Or, do you reposition students, depending upon what you are trying to accomplish? What can you do to arrange the chairs in your classroom so that students can learn more effectively?

The success of facilitative activities which appear in this book frequently depend upon how the students are grouped and the clarity of the tasks that are given. When students participate they are involved. Their interest is perked and they are motivated to stay on task. There is less opportunity for them to withdraw and become bored. As they become more involved, they are less likely to be disruptive or become a discipline problem. As they become move involved they like school better, learn more, and make your job easier.

Chapter 7
The Facilitative Procedures

Despite great differences among educational theorists, administrators, and the general public, affective education has been a popular subject of study for the past two decades. It was first introduced as part of the humanistic psychology movement, which started in the 1960s, and reached its zenith in the latter part of the 1970s when traditional ways of teaching were challenged. It was assumed that human potential could only be realized through development of one's inner resources and, subsequently, interpersonal relationships. It was further assumed that an awareness of self and others was a first step toward a positive self-concept, responsible decision-making, effective problem-solving, and personal growth.

For many people, affective education became synonymous with values clarification, self-knowledge, expression of emotions and feelings, and interpersonal experiences. Critics claimed that it was the introduction of "fun and games" into a traditional curriculum, which, admittedly, was too often unresponsive to the personal needs and interests of students. And, it was an infringement on personal rights and privacy where students were encouraged to self-disclose matters about themselves that were unrelated to the real curriculum—readin', writin', and 'rithmatic.

Supportive theorists countered by reminding us that education was more than an accumulation of facts and figures; it was more than storing and reciting information, more than the mastery of certain skills. Rather, it was preparing young people to become fully-functioning adults who were responsible citizens and who could make positive contributions in society. The social and emotional development of students was considered as essential as the academic curriculum.

Popular psychology followed by emphasizing self-development and positive belief in one's self. The jargon of the day became, "I'm OK—You're OK," and the goal was self-actualization. The objective was to "Feel Good About Yourself," "Be a Beautiful Person," and "Be a Caring and Sharing Person." It was believed that mental health was inherent in everyone and that each person was in control of one's own destiny. Being aware of and in control of the forces that affect one's self was the true mark of success.

Through the 1960s and 1970s group activities and techniques were developed to help people encounter themselves and others, to increase personal awareness, and to improve communication skills. Personal growth centers (e.g. National Training Laboratory— NTL; Esalen; Oasis; Kairos) became refuges for those who were seeking personal discovery and a better understanding of interpersonal relationships. It was new and exciting, as there was an atmosphere of oneness that led to creativity, understanding, cooperativeness, patience, and acceptance. It was not long before it was realized that everyone could benefit from self-development and that it was a good idea to begin early, when young people are in school. This would create a new-age philosophy of education, one which would be more self-enhancing and result in more caring and productive citizens.

Therefore, many of the same activities and techniques that were considered successful, or at least interesting, were proposed for teachers in their classrooms. Too many teachers, unfortunately, became quickly discouraged when they tried to apply some of the same methods and structured learning activities drawn from personal growth centers and sensitivity groups. They hoped that playing some group games would compensate for the missing affective component. However, these teachers quickly learned that the exercises in and of themselves were limited. Many teachers lacked both knowledge and skill, as well as experience. It was apparent that not all teachers were effective group leaders and that many of them had only a few vague notions about the principles of group dynamics and management. They needed to know more about how to build group cohesiveness, a climate for more participation, and the value of personalizing a learning experience.

For better or for worse, for several years there were many attempts to introduce affective education programs and activities into the school. School boards approved affective curricula, which had stated goals and which were lined up along side of the academic goals. They were considered parallel outcomes, and some said that affective education was the predecessor of academic knowledge. Others claimed that it was best viewed as an integrated part of all learning, not only a humanizing of education but a personalized and relevant approach. Regardless, it is definitely more than a few affective group activities.

Group activities or exercises are simply a means to an end. The end, in this case, is an increased opportunity for further self-exploration, understanding, and personal involvement. Group procedures and techniques are only a vehicle, and without an effective driver they will not help people reach their destinations. Teachers who know how to respond to children in facilitative ways, as described in the preceding chapters, tend to be most successful. They do not need to rely entirely on the structure of the group experience.

Those teachers who do not understand the value of the facilitative responses frequently report that their group activities fail and they erroneously conclude the procedures have no relevancy for use in the classroom. It is essential for teachers to understand how the facilitative responses, activities, and procedures work together. When these are combined and integrated into the regular classroom curriculum, personal and academic growth are both facilitated.

This chapter introduces some facilitative activities and procedures. They were selected to illustrate how activities might be used to:

1. elicit self-disclosure

2. encourage self-awareness and understanding

3. create opportunities for appraisal of self and others

4. enhance interpersonal communication skills

You may want to use these procedures as an integrated part of the regular curriculum. Or, you may prefer to set aside a certain time when the procedures will be used as part of a guidance program. On the other hand, you may want to use them as resource units to be drawn upon when a particular situation arises which needs more personal exploration and insight.

Pfeiffer and Jones (1979) concluded that facilitative activities such as those found in this chapter are like the folk music of human relations training. The origins of many group exercises are difficult to trace. They have been passed on by word of mouth, on bits of paper, and on unsigned, undated mimeographed sheets. It is not our intent to list all the available group activities and procedures that lend themselves to facilitating personal growth and effective learning. Rather, we wish to illustrate and discuss a few basic activities.

Section One:

Fantasy and Imagery

- ☐ The Creative Cave Experience
- ☐ Next to Nature
- ☐ A Body Awareness Experience
- ☐ The Head Trip
- ☐ The New You
- ☐ The Volunteer Experience
- ☐ Personal Paradise
- ☐ Water Treasure
- ☐ A Lonely Trip
- ☐ Freedom
- ☐ Inside
- ☐ Being a Puppet
- ☐ Fantasy Metaphors
- ☐ Traveling Companions
- ☐ Incomplete Fantasy
- ☐ The Exchange

Fantasy and imagination have received very little attention in education. Yet, through history they have been described as two of a human being's most powerful faculties. No doubt you have heard something similar to the statement, "One's potential is only limited by one's imagination?"

The Need for Fantasy and Imagination

Recent research suggests that it is necessary for us to dream in order to maintain our psychological equilibrium. Psychologists indicate that dreaming represents a method by which we work through some of our unconscious or subconscious mental processes. Research further indicates that if we are deprived of our dream activity, perhaps by being awakened at the instant we begin dreaming, we suffer psychologically. It is entirely possible that we also need to daydream, fantasize, and use our imaginations in order to function effectively. Sadly, daydreaming often has a negative connotation in our culture. How many times through the years were you told to "Stop daydreaming and get back to work!" or "Stop daydreaming and pay attention!" Thus, many people suffer guilt feelings because of their daydreaming activities.

Radio programs force us to exercise our fantasy and imagination with their adventure and action. Television, on the other hand, presents detailed visual situations that engage us in someone else's fantasy and there is less need to develop our own.

Subjective experiences, especially those involving imagery, are experiences that both children and adults enjoy. Fantasy experiences free us to be ourselves—to discover ourselves through make-believe situations. We have a need for such inner experiences and we actively seek methods of involving ourselves in them.

Many adults as well as children use unnatural methods to gain fantasy experiences. Alcohol and drugs are the most common artificial methods used by many people to free themselves from their inhibitions. But, at the same time, these artificial ingredients also suppress the senses. With some systematic structure, natural imagery and fantasy can provide rewarding personal experiences for an individual, many times leading to insight, control, and a reduction of stress.

The Power of Fantasy and Imagination

We all live with the notion and hope that at least a part of our fantasy world will be realized someday. The goals of imagination and reality are not necessarily separate. Through talking about our fantasies, we externalize them and they can become more realistic goals and motivational forces. The verbalization of a fantasy enables us to get a picture of action that is needed to make something happen.

Imagination and fantasy can be very powerful in everyday behavior. For example, there are many professional golfers who use their imagination to play an entire golf match in their mind before the actual tournament takes place. They envision themselves on the golf course—feeling relaxed and confident, seeing the fairway, addressing and hitting the ball perfectly, hearing noises, walking to the ball, and seeing people as they enjoy the success. To them, it is not just a daydream. They expect such practice in their minds to help them behave accordingly when they are on the course.

If we were to place a 5 x 5 inch, 25-foot long wooden beam on the floor, most of us could walk the length of it without falling. However, if the same plank were raised 25 feet, most of us would refuse to walk it. Our imagination would likely dominate and we would have a fear of falling. If we were to cross the plank at that height, we would have to control our imagination, actually use its power to get us across.

Psychologists and hypnotherapists report that most people, via their imaginations, can develop glove anesthesia. Glove anesthesia is the condition where there is no sensation in one's hand from the tips of the fingers to the wrist. With systematic structuring of the experience, subjects are conditioned, through their imagination, to visualize their hands as pieces of wood or covered with lead gloves. With such mental conditioning, hands become insensitive to pain.

Some psychotherapists utilize imagery in their work. For example, they can relax an excessively anxious patient by guiding the person through imaginary anxiety evoking situations. The human body cannot be both relaxed and anxious at the same time. Thus, the patient, in imaginary simulations, goes through the anxiety evoking situations while being totally relaxed, much like the professional golfer mentioned before. With this type of conditioning, relaxation and coping skills will be paired with the original anxiety provoking situation. There is considerable evidence that this type of therapy (learning) is successful.

Contrary to popular belief, the power of the imagination is not similar to "positive thinking" or "willpower." If you were at this moment to "will" or "positive think" your mouth to water, it would not occur. However, if you would imagine your favorite type of food (perhaps one of your favorite meals), your mouth might begin to salivate. It is a matter of using your imagination.

You and Your Imagination

We think in images. As you read the following words, what do you see? A — large — animal — with — four — legs — with — a — saddle — on — its — back. Did you form an image of a specific animal? Did you think or say "horse" to yourself? What color was the animal? Did any other senses come into play—smell, auditory, touch?

Now, see what happens as you read the word "horse" in this paragraph. Try the same thing with other words such as house, car, tree, bear, cow, and so forth. Imagery goes beyond printed or spoken symbols. Look at the following words: happy — gay — sad — laughing — fast. Did you realize some sort of image as you read these words?

What does the word "nomel" mean to you? Probably, there is little associative value for you. Say the word to yourself a few times. It is probably a non-sense term for you; therefore it elicits no mental images. Now spell the word (nomel) backwards. Ah-ha, Lemon! Now the word makes sense and you probably have a mental image. Learning takes place through the process of imagery conditioning to particular stimuli. As we hear a word over and over, we condition ourselves to particular stimuli. Thus, as we hear a word repeatedly, we condition ourselves to respond to that word via a mental image or symbol with thoughts, with feelings, or with actions that have been conditioned to that particular word or symbol. Imagery goes beyond symbols. For example, you may not have only seen a yellow lemon, but you may have experienced a sour taste which may have made you pucker your lips a little.

Let us now take a hypothetical situation and see how the principle of imagery conditioning applies to you. Let's assume (imagine if you will) that you are three or four years old, and you're learning to read and to talk.

Perhaps you were shown pictures of many different animals and the names were spelled out in large letters under the pictures. Repeatedly, you were shown a picture, for instance, of a horse and the word "horse" was used simultaneously. When possible, an actual horse was pointed out to you and again the word "horse" was repeated.

After many such experiences, you responded to the sound of the word with either a mental image of the printed word, the picture of the horse, or maybe by actually seeing a horse in your imagination. You became conditioned to respond to this stimulus with mental images of your own. For example, some people upon hearing the word horse, will see the letters h-o-r-s-e, while others see the image of a horse.

Learning basically is a process of conditioning responses through imagery and we tend to behave according to the images we conjure up. If children have images of themselves as failures, they tend to fail. If they have an image of the teacher as a mean person, they feel threatened and may withdraw. If they describe themselves as "I'm no good," they live and act accordingly. If they imagine themselves in a fearful situation, they respond with anxiety. However, if the images of themselves and the teacher are more positive, they probably will be more likely to enjoy themselves and their work with the teacher.

Implications for the Facilitative Teacher

One of the authors has experimented with underachievers using structured imagination activities. Through structured imagery experiences, they visualize themselves achieving and being successful. This seems to have a positive effect on their behaviors. That is, many of these underachievers have attempted to carry out that which they saw themselves doing in their imaginations.

We are a sight-oriented culture. "I'll *see* you around." "I'll *see* you later." "Do you *see* what I'm saying?" "Do you *see* the point?" However, other senses are an important part of our lives and our learning too. When the eyes are closed, we obtain the maximum benefits from structured imagination. With the eyes closed we shut off distracting stimuli which interfere with some input and its retention. When the eyes are closed, sensory receptors come keenly into operation. Other senses, such as hearing (e.g., blind people can have a better sense of hearing than sighted people), touch, tasting, smelling—with a little bit of practice—become much more sensitive when the eyes are closed. The use of the senses are too frequently avoided in classroom learning processes.

There are many ways that imagination might be used in the academic learning process. For example, some teachers have used imagery procedures to help children learn mathematics. Children close their eyes and each of the numbers takes on a very special meaning for the children through the use of their imagination. The script for imaginary events, i.e., one which children might use to learn numbers, should be written in advance so that it could be easily read aloud or taped for use with students. The following is an excerpt taken from a tape developed by a third grade teacher who used it to teach the multiplication tables:

> *(Students' eyes are closed and the tape has soft music in the background.)* "Now, visualize in your mind a brightly colored 7. It is becoming very bright now and it is quietly dancing over to the number 6. It softly taps the 6 six times. One tap, two taps, three, four, five, and six. Slowly, in a circle next to the number 6 is appearing a new number. Can you make it out? It's becoming clear. You can see it. It's a 42. The 6 smiles at you and says, Well, button my shoe, 7 times 6 is 42.

Imagination experiences can be overstructured. You could observe in the above excerpt that the teacher did not indicate the color of the seven. This was left to each student's imagination. If you refer to flowers during a sequence for taping, avoid giving the type or color unless you have a special purpose and know that the person has knowledge of them (a reference point). If you must mention color in your sequence, mention it before the noun. For instance, say, "There is a red house," rather than, "There is a house. It is red." Likewise, you may not need to indicate the direction of the wind or a running stream.

Too many clues cause internal confusion. For example, as you now read the word "stream," you may conjure up an image that also includes the direction the water is running. If you had your eyes closed and your stream was running right to left and the script said it was running left to right, you would be temporarily confused. While this is not a critical problem, as our minds are resilient and will quickly make the adjustment, it is a little awkward, jerky, and the flow of the experience is interrupted.

Fantasy experiences that are too long should also be avoided. For elementary students, 6-8 minutes is probably as long as you will want to go. Longer sequences may have them lose their concentration and develop an unrelated scenario, or actually put them to sleep. After all, in most of these experiences, their eyes will be closed and their bodies relaxed. Older students, of course, can participate in somewhat longer experiences, but they too tend to drift into another mind adventure if a structured or guided fantasy is too long.

An easy method of preparing students for imaginary activities is to have them briefly close their eyes and imagine a few things that they can easily think about. For example, you might ask them to imagine that they have just taken a bite of a crisp apple. The bite was almost too large for their mouth. Then ask them to imagine that they are finally chewing it up and swallowing.

Can you imagine the smell of ammonia? The taste of a sour lemon? Walking barefooted over marbles? Have your students try these for warm-ups. Also, remind them that they should be in the scene, doing it, rather than being a spectator and only seeing themselves in action. As they get into the scene, they smell things, taste things, hear things—they are there!

Let your students know that they should not judge their fantasies while they are experiencing them. It is best just to go with a fantasy and let it happen. Also, it is important that you remind others not to play analyst and analyze or interpret another person's fantasies (see Chapter III) when experiences are discussed.

Before you utilize any of the following activities, first prepare your students for them. One of the first things you should talk about is that everyone will be asked to close their eyes. Some students may be hesitant to do this at first. Gain assurance from everyone in the class that all will close their eyes and keep them closed during the experience. Some students become embarrassed if they have their eyes closed while others observe them. If you tape your imaginary exercises, you might assure the students that you also will be closing your eyes and joining in the experience.

Guidelines for Guided Imagery

Here are some basic guidelines that can help you with the imagery activities:

1. Use imaginary examples to set the mood. Ask students to get into the experience—to be there. Tell them to go along with the experience, relax, and enjoy it. There are no correct or incorrect visual pictures to see.

2. Talk about the importance of keeping eyes closed.

3. Help them relax before beginning an activity, perhaps with a few deep breaths.

4. Use a soft, soothing voice when guiding them.

5. Tape or write out the words of the activity beforehand.

6. Use soft music as background, if possible, but don't let it detract from the experience or be the determining factor for using guided imagery.

7. Use words in the narration that connote texture and that utilize all the senses.

8. Allow ample time for discussion. Don't interpret a student's fantasy, nor permit others to do it. This is not psychoanalysis, nor should that ever be implied.

9. Use the high facilitative responses during discussion to promote sharing and acceptance of experiences.

10. Choose a time of the day when you will not be interrupted. You might hang a "Do Not Disturb" sign on your classroom door. A place free from outside noise is ideal, but not essential. Students can learn to shut out the distractions when they are properly prepared and have had some practice.

Fantasy and Imagery Activities
The Creative Cave Experience

Purpose:
To develop creativity and to stimulate the imagination.

Procedure:
You might tape the following fantasy, but the script could also be read in person. Regardless, speak softly, slowly, distinctly, and in a soothing voice. The tape might include soft music in the background.

1. Ask everyone to close their eyes and to keep them closed until the voice on the tape says to open them.

2. Play the tape (or read the script).

3. After you've completed the exercise, give the students an opportunity to discuss their experiences. Be certain that all students get an opportunity, if desired, to tell about their experiences.If you have a large class, you might break them up into small groups or triads for discussion. The discussion following an activity, where each student is facilitated to disclose feelings and ideas concerning the experience is a significant aspect of this activity. No judging, interpreting, or advising.

4. Use the high facilitative responses (Chapter III) in the discussion.

The Experience:
Close your eyes and get in the most comfortable position you can find. Put your hands and your feet where they are the most comfortable and relax. As I talk to you, imagine that with each and every breath you are becoming more and more relaxed. Now, rest your head, take a deep breath (pause) and hear my words. Listen. Let any noises around you fade away....

All that is important now is that you relax. Just let yourself go, sink down (pause).Keep breathing deeply—in and out. Now, here in this very comfortable position, feeling very pleasant, imagine that your whole body has gone limp. Let any tension that you have in your body drain downward, down through your legs and out to the floor. You feel very loose, now, very tranquil. The feeling of looseness is all around you, peaceful, very calm and relaxed. You find yourself becoming even more and more relaxed now with each and every breath.

You see a very beautiful field and you are walking barefoot across it toward a small woods off in the distance (pause). As you approach the woods, you can see the leaves on the trees and you can feel the green soft grass between your toes. There is a slight breeze... it brushes gently against your face. It's very pleasant. It feels so good to be so close to nature.

Walking on, you come to the top of a small hill on the edge of the woods. You are standing in the grass. The grass is very green, soft, like velvet to your feet... so delicate, so very soft and very delicate. You can feel it as it touches your feet (pause). You see beautiful flowers in bloom and smell their fragrances.

As you stand here on this small hill, looking out, you notice a small stream. The water is rippling slowly over some small stones in the stream and you can see the mist as it rises gently and slowly from the water. It is a beautiful sight and you're feeling so happy and pleasant.

Now, as you look upstream, you see a small white duck floating on top of the water, floating downstream toward you (pause). The duck is very calm and peaceful—just floating downstream. The duck has not a care in the world (pause). Now it is floating directly in front of you... floating downstream now. Your eyes follow the duck. It is getting further and further downstream, getting smaller. Now, it goes around a small bend and is out of sight (pause).

Move away from the stream now and walk back toward the woods. You can see the trees. Each tree becomes more and more vivid as you become more and more relaxed.... As you walk along here in the woods, think about how beautiful and peaceful it is, how good it is to be this close to nature.

As you walk on you see the shadows of the trees cast on the ground below. You look up and see the sun twinkling through the trees (pause). So peaceful. You walk on now and you come to a clearing at the end of the woods. There before you is a pond. The water is clear, so clear and quiet. It's not moving at all. It is like a mirror and you can see the reflections of the trees in the water (pause). You stop beside the pond, look down and put your hand in the water.... You can now feel the water on your hand.

Take your hand out of water and gaze into this beautiful, clear pond. You begin to see your own reflection. It is becoming very clear now. You can see yourself. You are smiling. You can see what you are wearing. You are very relaxed. (Pause for 5 to 10 seconds.) Now, move away from the pond and walk across the beautiful field. In front of you there is a small mountain. As you gaze at the mountain you notice an opening—an opening leading into a cave (pause).

You decide to go into the cave. As you enter the cave, you can see the rock formations, feel the moistness, and in the background you can hear the drip, drip of water. The cave gradually leads down deeper into the ground. It is very quiet and peaceful here in the cave. You make your way down deeper in to the cave. You stop to take a breath and relax. You are relaxing more with every moment, every breath... every passing moment... relaxing more. It is so quiet and peaceful here. You look there toward the back of the cave and notice a bright light coming from an opening at the back of the cave. You make your way through this opening now, going into another section of the cave. It is full of light and it is a very beautiful area of the cave (pause). There in front of you is a statue. A statue (pause). Suddenly, you are aware that this statue can talk and is talking to you. Listen to what it says. Talk to the statue now.

(Allow at least two minutes here. If you use music, let it play on.) Now, I am going to ask you to make a decision concerning the statue. Will you bring the statue out with you, or will you leave it behind in the cave? You must decide now. You have just a moment. (Pause for about 60 seconds.) Okay, make your way back out of the cave, out into the sunlight (pause).

Now, at the count of three you will open your eyes and you will feel alert and refreshed. One, two, you're becoming more alert. Three, gently stretch and open your eyes.

Discussion:
The following excerpts are taken from discussions of the Creative Cave Experience.

1. A Third Grade Male

Student:
When the voice said statue, I saw Julius Caesar. He was just standing there all stony and cold. Then the tape said he could talk so I took an ice pick and chipped him out of that stone. He smiled real big and said 'Thank you.' We started talking and he told me about olden days and what it was like then.

Teacher:
It was exciting to you (feeling focused response).

Student:
Yeah, and he told me about these witches and he got all embarrassed.

Teacher:
Embarrassed (clarification).

Student:
Well, wouldn't you be embarrassed if you told somebody you knew a witch (laughing)?

Teacher:
His embarrassment was sort of humorous to you (clarification).

Student:
Oh, it wasn't really funny, at least not to him. But I think that's one reason why he didn't want to come out with me. He said he had to be where it was cool. He didn't want sunshine. I said, 'okay, maybe I'll see you again if the teacher plays the tape again.'

Teacher:
You didn't want to force him to come out with you and you'd like to visit him again someday (clarification, summary).

2. A Fourth Grade Male

Student:
I felt so good there by the pond that I just didn't want to leave it, so I went fishing. (This type of experience is rare, but it does occur and a student should understand that this is acceptable).

Teacher:
You felt so comfortable that you just couldn't leave the pond, so you did what you wanted to (A feeling-focused response).

3. A Sixth Grade Female

Student:
I saw the Statue of Liberty. I guess that's because I'm a Woman's Libber (laughingly). No, seriously, she was trying to hum but she had a straw in her mouth and that made it hard to do.

Teacher:
Your conversation was about her humming and it was funny for you (A clarification and feeling-focused response).

Student:
Yeah, she said that she didn't know what she was doing in this cave when she should be out in the harbor directing ship traffic. I told her that was okay because I goof off too sometimes. She said that she had a headache all the time because of all those people stomping around in her head (laughing).

Teacher:
You let her know that she was okay because you were both sort of alike (A clarifying response).

Student:
I wanted to bring her out but the opening wasn't big enough.

Teacher:
And that was frustrating (Feeling-focused response).

Student:
Yeah, it was.

4. A Tenth Grade Male

Student:
I saw a statue of Jesus on the cross and I couldn't hardly make it out, and then you said he could talk and it all became so real. I really don't know how long we talked but we talked about poverty, war, and things like that. It was so vivid that at first I was sort of scared. I saw the robe and everything. And, you know before you said I had the choice of whether or not to bring him out, I had made the choice. I brought him out with me.

Teacher:
The experience was significant to you and it was as if you were really there (A clarification).

Some children and adults see statues of themselves. It is common for adults to see Jesus or the Virgin Mary. Others see their parents or a favorite relative. The statue of David is also a favorite among adults. Perhaps this is because they are well-known statues and people are familiar with them, a reference point in which to project their fantasy. Discussions following the guided fantasy provide an opportunity to facilitate open, honest communication, in an atmosphere where the facilitative conditions are developed.

Next to Nature

Purpose:
This guided imagery is basically a warm-up experience. It is designed to interest your students in the use of imagination.

Procedure:
Use the same general procedures as for the Creative Cave Experience.

The Experience:
Close your eyes now. Relax. Take a deep breath and breath it out slowly. Relax and just let yourself go. Breath again, and relax more with each breath. Let any noises you may hear just fade away.

Imagine that you are walking in a forest on a sunny day. See the trees. Look carefully at them (pause). There are light, fleecy clouds over head (pause). You feel free. As you walk along, you notice flowers... shrubs... trees... and patterns of light as the sun shines down through the branches. You feel a slight breeze.... It brushes lightly against your face. You hear the sound of water bubbling over the rocks in a nearby small stream.

Now, you are walking down a small path in the forest.... As you follow the path, you come to a clearing, and there to the front of you is a small river. There is a small canoe pulled up on the shore. You are walking toward the canoe. You step in, push off easily and effortlessly (pause). There is a nice soft pillow there at one end of the canoe and you lean back as the boat lazily drifts along.... You notice the trees on the shore as they fade into the distance.

You're drifting down the small stream. Lean back onto the soft cushion, just drifting. Now, look up at the soft white clouds over head. There in the distance you can see and hear a tiny airplane and as you watch, the airplane slowly, in white smoke, spells out your name in giant letters across the sky (pause).

You lay there in the canoe, enjoying what you are seeing, smelling, and hearing. Now, reach over the side of the canoe and put your hand in the water. The water feels chilly. It's somewhat numbing (pause). Put your other hand in the water over the other side of the canoe. On this side the water is warm (pause).

Okay, now open your eyes on the count of three ... 1... 2... 3....

Discussion:

The following excerpts were taken from discussions of the Next To
Nature Experience as it occurred in a fifth grade class:

1. Male Student

   Student:
   *My hand really got cold when I put it in the water. I ac-
   tually felt it!*

   Teacher:
   *It was as if you were there and you seemed surprised that
   you felt the chill (Feeling-focused).*

   Student:
   *Yeah, and then I put the other hand in and the water was
   nice and warm. It was really different.*

   Teacher:
   So, you could sense the difference (Clarification).

2. Female Student

   Student:
   *My head was on a soft, satin pillow and I was almost
   asleep when I suddenly looked up to the sky and right
   there was my name, all spelled out in these great, big letters.*

   Teacher:
   *You were relaxed and then became alert when you saw
   your name. What else did you experience during the fantasy trip (Feeling focused/open-ended question)?*

   Student:
   *I was afraid when the river got real narrow. I thought
   snakes might drop out of the low hanging trees into the
   canoe.*

   Teacher:
   *That part of the experience was scary for you (Feeling-
   focused).*

A Body Awareness Experience

Purpose:

The purpose is to increase body awareness through imagination. This is also a unique way to relax the body. It encourages students to use their other-than-sight senses.

Procedure:

1. Lead a discussion in which the following ideas are conveyed to set the stage for the experience. As human beings, we are sensitive by nature. As children we use our senses in play and exploration. But, as we grow older there is more of an emphasis on using the thinking (or cognitive) part of ourselves and less on continuing our sensory development. Thus, we learn "non sense." Our lack of sensitivity can create an imbalance between thinking and feeling. It helps to fine-tune all our senses and use them with our intellect.

2. Play the tape (see previously suggested procedures).

The Experience:

Close your eyes and relax. Let the tension drain from you. Just relax and follow your thoughts. Follow your thoughts just the way they are right now. There's no need to try to change them. Follow your thoughts for one minute (pause). Now, for a moment, become aware of how you feel. Be aware of what you are feeling now... your sensations as they are just now (pause).

Without any movement, shift your attention to your feet. Become conscious, be aware of what your feet are resting on (pause).... Now, concentrate on your right foot. Be aware of the big toe... now your second toe..., the middle toe..., the next toe... and finally, the little toe on your right foot (pause). Now, be aware of the top of your right foot, the curvature (pause).

Shift your awareness to your left foot. Be aware of the big toe on the left foot (pause), the next toe, the middle toe, the fourth toe, and again the little toe. Now, without moving your feet, shift your awareness to the top of your left foot (pause).

Now, feel, experience, and be aware of your ankles (pause). Relax.

Shift your attention and be aware of your right knee, the roundness, the firmness, experience your right knee (pause). Now, shift your awareness to your left knee. Experience it.

Experience both thighs (pause). Your hips (pause). Your buttocks (pause). Be aware of that which is supporting you. Be aware of what your buttocks are against (pause).

Shift your awareness to your stomach. Is it tight? Where is it tight? Relax and let the tightness go (pause).

Now, be aware of your chest. Experience it (pause). Be aware of your back and be aware of what your back is against (pause).

Now shift your awareness to your right hand, and without any movement, be aware of your right thumb. Be aware of your fingers and what they are resting on (pause). Move to your left hand. Sense your thumb and your fingers (pause).

Now, be aware of your left elbow (pause). Now, your right elbow (pause).

Experience your shoulders and let them move just a little. Move your shoulders up and down. Be aware of your neck... your lips... your tongue... your nose... your eyes... your forehead. See your forehead... be aware of it.

Now, visualize your lungs. See them as they fill up with air... as they expel the air (pause). Experience and be aware of your breathing... hear your breathing. Be aware of the people around you. Hear the sounds around you (pause).

The Head Trip

Purpose:
To reveal part of one's self-concept. Most of us realize that there are many sides to a personality, (e.g., one part is revealed when we answer the phone pleasantly and another when we are irritated). This exercise permits students to experience "another self."

Procedure:
Use the same procedures as the Creative Cave Experience.

The Experience:

Now close you eyes and let your body relax. Just sort of sink down. Let your head go where it wants to go. With each and every breath, relax more and more. Let everything go from your mind, just let your mind go blank. You are feeling calm, relaxed.

As you remain now in this relaxed state, follow my words. First, imagine that you can see yourself as you are right now. Let yourself see you. Whether you are sitting or lying down, you are looking at you as you are right now... there with your eyes closed. See yourself as you are right now.

Now, visualize your self in miniature. So small that you are less than an inch in height. You are very small... a miniature you (pause). See yourself now.

The image becomes vivid as you see yourself... less than an inch in height... very much alive, yet so small, so tiny. Now, you are that miniature self and you are walking into your mouth... walking into your mouth (pause). You stand there inside... in semi-darkness... sensing the moisture. Looking around, you now look upward. There in the roof of your mouth is an open trap door. You can see that it is well lighted in that part of your head. There is a small ladder leading upward to the lighted opening. Remain relaxed and climb the ladder now. Climb the ladder and enter that part of your head. You are almost there. Now, look around. What do you see? (Pause for about 30 seconds.) As you look toward the back of your head you see a small door that leads to another part of your head (pause). Open the door. It is semi-dark inside. Enter and close the door behind you.

You can make out an image in the semi-darkness. That image is another you, but a different you... another self. How is the other self dressed? How does it look? It is now talking to you. How does it sound? What is it saying? ...Now, talk to your other self. Carry on a conversation. (Pause about 30 seconds.) Now, you must decide whether to bring your other self out with you. What will you do? (pause) It is time to leave now. OK, now count to three and slowly open your eyes. (Use "wake-up" for first experience.)

Discussion:

The following excerpts are from classroom discussions concerning the Head Trip Experience.

1. A Kindergarten Male

Student:

I was a little elf and went inside my mouth.

Teacher:
What was it like (opened-ended question)?

Student:
All dark and yukky.

Teacher:
It made you uneasy to be there (feeling focused).

2. Seventh Grade Female

Student:
The ladder was all shiny and wet. My hands kept slipping and I didn't want to go, but I finally made it to the top.

Teacher:
You were reluctant to go to the top part of your head (Feeling-focused).

Student:
Yeah, but I did see my other self up there.

Teacher:
What would you like to share about that part of the experience (open-ended question)?

3. Eleventh Grade Male

Student:
Man, I wasn't about to bring my other self out with me—no way!

Teacher:
What else can you tell us about that (open-ended question)?

Student:
Well, if you would've seen how he looked, well, you wouldn't have wanted to see him.

Teacher:
Something about the other self was really different. (clarification).

Student:
(Laughing) Yeah, he had two horns, like a devil.

The teacher is attempting to focus on the student as a person before talking about the event-the actual fantasy experience.

The New You

Purpose:
This activity encourages students to confront an undesirable, personal trait of their choice.

Procedure:
Use the same procedures as for the Creative Cave Experience.

The Experience:
Now that your eyes are closed, let your body relax. Imagine yourself sinking down... just let yourself go. Take a deep breath (pause) and listen to what I say. I am going to count from five down to zero and you will be able to see the numbers. With each number you become more and more relaxed...

Now, picture the number five, think about it, imagine that you are tracing it with your finger.... Now, you see the number four, it becomes more and more vivid... trace it. Picture the three, and you become more relaxed.... Two, you feel peaceful, content.... One, just let yourself go.... Now, picture the zero and take another deep breath (pause) letting it out slowly, completely relaxed now. Visualize the zero as being a magic carpet... get on.

You are gliding peacefully and slowly.... You feel the air brushing lightly against your face.... You come to a beautiful forest and you land there. You are now going for a walk down a trail in the woods....

You see the trees... smell the fragrances of the forest.... Each tree becomes more and more vivid as you become more relaxed. As you walk down the path, you sense how beautiful and peaceful it is... how good it is to be this close to nature.... As you walk on, you can see the shadows cast on the ground below you.... You can see the sun twinkling between the trees... feeling so close to nature makes you feel so relaxed... so peaceful.

As you walk on you come to a clearing at the end of the trail. There before you is a beautiful, quiet pond. It's like a mirror and you can see the reflections of the trees in it. As you stop beside the pond and gaze into the water, you see your own reflection (pause). The image becomes very clear... you see what you are wearing. As you stand there and look down you see all of you in the pond. You see you.

Imagine that this pond is magic... a place where you can discard any habit or personality trait you have that you want to get rid of... something that you dislike about yourself, something that you would like to change. Take a moment to decide what you wish to discard (pause).

As you continue to gaze at your reflection in the pond, you see yourself as you are with this part of you that you wish to rid yourself of (pause). The image is becoming clear.... Then, someone drops a rock in to the water and the ripples made by the rock wash away the old image.... The unwanted part is being washed away in the water (pause).

As the water stills again, you see your new image....You see a new you. You are relaxed, smiling about the new image. You feel changed. You are different now (pause). Just let yourself be at ease with this change. (pause)

In a moment we will stop and open our eyes. (pause) I'll count to 3 and then you will open your eyes 1-2 stretch gently—5 open your eyes.

We are getting ready to stop. Stop now and slowly open your eyes. Your eyes are open now.

The Volunteer Experience

Purpose:

This exercise assists individuals in clarifying for themselves and others some of their inner conflicts in decision-making.

Procedure:

1. Begin by asking for some volunteers. Don't tell the group what you want the volunteers to do; rather, make it a little mysterious, perhaps emphasizing that it will be challenging. Take a little time to let the suspense build, before saying, "Okay, Stop!"

2. Have all participants close their eyes and ask them to be quiet and listen carefully.

3. Read the following exercise.

The Experience:

Make yourself as comfortable as you can and close your eyes. Take a deep breath and relax.

Now that your eyes are closed, I want you to focus on the experience you've just had. I just asked for some volunteers and each of you had to decide what to do. Should you volunteer or not? Now, imagine that there are two people in your head, one arguing that you should volunteer and the other arguing against it.

Listen to their arguments for a minute, as each tries to convince you what to do. (pause)

Now, let them continue trying to convince you, but this time they are not talking. What are they doing? How are they trying to convince you what to do? Watch them. (pause)

Now they stop and leave you to make your own decision (pause), then count to 3, open your eyes 1-2-3.

You see, I really didn't need any volunteers. I wanted you to think about the arguments that would be used to influence your actions. What happened when I asked you to let the two people argue and try to convince you what to do? How did their voices sound? How were they dressed? Was one bigger than the other? What happened when they didn't use spoken words. How did they try to convince you? Who was winning when I asked you to stop?

Personal Paradise

Procedure:
Ask everyone to think of a very pleasant and relaxing place (or time) in their life. For some people it will be a particular beach, woods, field, or perhaps a trip to grandmother's house.

Next, place them into dyads and ask them to talk about this place—this kind of paradise. Have them reconstruct a picture of an event at this place. Were there trees, snow, sand, or water in the picture?

Then, have everyone in the group close their eyes and imagine themselves being in their personal paradise and doing something that they would like to do.

Water Treasure

Procedure:
Lead the class in fantasizing about an underwater treasure hunt. Take the students on an adventure which leads to an old treasure chest. Have them open it. Stop and have them tell what they saw.

A Lonely Trip

Procedure:
In this experience the students are asked to fantasize about what it is like to feel lonely and then, still in fantasy, they go to a place where they feel they would be most lonely. What is it like for them there? The sights, sounds, and feelings.

Freedom

Procedure:
Students are asked to fantasize about what it is like to feel completely free. They go to a place where they feel they would be most free. What would it be like? Who would be there? Who would not be there? How much time would they like to spend there?

Inside

Procedure:
Have students imagine themselves inside something—a cocoon, a large bubble, a satin bag, or a velvet-lined box. What were the feelings?

Being a Puppet

Procedure:
Have students imagine that they are puppets with strings attached to all parts of their bodies. A good friend is the puppeteer and is having them do a pleasant task.

Fantasy Metaphors

Procedure:
After breaking the class into groups, have students fantasize about what animal, bird, building, geometric figure, plant, color and so forth they would like to be.

Traveling Companions

Procedure:
Ask members of the class to imagine that they are going on a trip to a far away island and to select any four people they would want to go with them. Or, you are in a hospital, seriously ill. If you had your choice, what people, excluding relatives, would visit you often? What made you choose these people?

Incomplete Fantasy

Procedure:

Ask the students to close their eyes and to listen carefully to the story that you will read to them, such as those that follow. They are to finish the story:

> *You are lying in the warm sun inside a brick courtyard.*
> *You can hear the birds singing when suddenly....*

Now, allow time for students to discuss their fantasies. Some may want to write their responses. Here is another example:

> *You are taking a trip on a cross-country bus. The bus*
> *passes through a small town. As you ride down a narrow*
> *street, you're looking out the window and you see....*

The Exchange

Procedure:

Members of the group are asked to imagine that they are shopping at a place where only intangibles are in stock. Any intangible, such as love, honesty, intelligence, and so forth may be bartered. That is, something the individual already has must be left in exchange. If one wishes to acquire honesty, that student might trade good health, joy of living, intelligence, and so forth.

Section Two:

Learning About
Feelings and Behaviors

- ☐ **Dear Abby**
- ☐ **Problem Moments**
- ☐ **Pantomiming Emotions**
- ☐ **Feelings Tally**
- ☐ **Group Pictures**

- ☐ **Unfair Debate**
- ☐ **Sociodrama**
- ☐ **Feelings and Music**
- ☐ **Inside/Outside Circle**
- ☐ **Go-Around**

Guided imagery and fantasy activities can help students to tune into themselves more, to become more aware of their senses and the power of their minds. It is through discussion, however, that the experiences are shared and their personal meanings are explored. Discussions are more relevant and productive when students know how to talk about their thoughts and ideas, and their feelings and behaviors.

Feelings and behaviors are related. We often take note of what people do and how they act, but are less inclined to notice the cues which suggest what people are feeling. Too often feelings are ignored; yet, they are tied closely to behaviors. People perceive, feel, and act. They also act and, subsequently, have feelings. If students are to be more in control of themselves and to be more responsible for their behaviors, then they must know more about what they are experiencing—feeling.

The concept of feelings classes was first introduced by Faust (1968). In the beginning, it was assumed that feelings classes should be used primarily in the elementary school, to help children build a vocabulary and to become more aware of themselves and others. Many educators, however, began to recognize that what a student is feeling, or experiencing, is an integral part of the school curriculum, regardless of grade level.

Most curricula focus on the cognitive or intellectual factors, with little attention to how feelings are related to learning and the way people behave. Yet, thinking, feeling, and doing are so interrelated that it is inconceivable that learning can take place without all three components being present. When one of the components is ignored, learning is less efficient and effective. Awareness of self and others, therefore, begins with learning more about the nature of feelings. The major objectives of a feelings class are:

1. To help students become aware that feelings exist. This involves a sensitizing experience for students. Only after students are sensitized to their feelings can they learn to effectively deal with them.

2. To help students become aware that all people possess, at all times, all kinds of feelings. That is, students need to learn that they have feelings in common with other students and that they are not alone in their experiences. Learning that others also feel the same way tends to reduce feelings of inadequacy or guilt that so often cause excessive anxiety and ineffective learning.

3. To help students become more aware that feelings are neither bad nor ugly. Students learn that one need not act out every feeling. All of us learn to inhibit certain behaviors or channel certain feelings in socially effective ways. There is no need to ignore or to deny feelings, even those that are labeled in our society or culture as undesirable. Ignoring or denying feelings creates defensiveness and distortion that can only lead to ineffective thinking and behavior patterns.

4. To help students learn socially effective ways of expressing feelings. Some behaviors are unacceptable to most of society. We must recognize that as human beings we have a wide range of feelings and that some of them can generate behaviors that society does not sanction. Helping students recognize their feelings and helping them channel them into socially effective behaviors is an essential aspect in all learning.

These objectives can be met through regular classroom activities. They may be scheduled for 20 to 30 minutes each day. Yet, many opportunities arise for "timely teaching" where a teacher can facilitate the exploration of feelings as they are related to a spontaneous classroom experience, idea, or personal incident.

With young children, for example, a teacher may request that students bring pictures from magazines or newspapers that show a special feeling. Or, the teacher may have a set of pictures which are particularly appropriate for introducing the exploration of some feelings. The pictures might illustrate happiness or perhaps portray anger, fear, affection, loneliness, and so forth.

One teacher showed a first grade class some pictures that showed people doing things. The class was asked if they could tell what was happening in each of the pictures. The students were encouraged to think of what might have taken place before a picture was taken, how the people were feeling, and what might happen later. The teacher inquired as to how the children could tell what the people were feeling. The pleasant and unpleasant feeling words which seem to be present in the pictures were listed on the chalk board. With the teacher's help, the class focused on the nonverbal cues which had led to conclusions about what the people in the pictures were experiencing.

After the discussion, the children were encouraged to draw pictures that dealt with the feelings of anger, which were portrayed in one picture. In other instances, stories might have been written, model clay used, or plays might have been acted out. By helping the class in an exploration of the feelings, the teacher was providing a firsthand experience where the children could eventually discuss their own experiences.

The teacher in the last case followed this general sequence of questions, with appropriate use of other high facilitative responses in the discussion.

1. What do you think is happening in this picture? What do you think took place just before the picture was taken? How do you think things will turn out?

2. What are some words that might be used to describe the feelings people are having in the picture? (List them on the board.)

3. Let's draw a picture that expresses these feelings. (Point to the word "anger.")

5. Can you tell me about a time in your life when you felt angry? Have you ever known anyone in your life who felt angry? What did they do? What did you do?

6. What are some ways in which people can release their angry feelings without hurting others? All the ways the children can think of are considered.

A discussion then takes place as to which of the ones seem to be the most socially effective and least harmful to others. These steps are basic to any feelings class experience, although the medium for introducing feelings will change. Moreover, these steps are effective at different age levels. A high school English class might do a similar thing, perhaps through a written theme or play.

Feelings are an inextricable part of the learning process and any effort to encourage students to become more aware of their feelings, their total self, enhances their learning and development. In this respect, feelings classes might also be labeled an important part of a developmental or preventive guidance program.

Many children in need of counseling and guidance are not aware of their own feelings. Because they fail to see how feelings are related to their behaviors, they are less responsible, frequently get into trouble, and blame others for their problems. On the other hand, students who feel they are understood, that they are valued, that their feelings are important, tend to identify more positively with others, and consequently, have less need to be negative towards them.

As students experience feelings classes, they tend to:

1. have access to their feelings—an awareness of them;

2. integrate their feelings with more cognitive types of intellectual processes;

3. become relatively unafraid of their feelings;

4. be relatively guilt-free regarding their feelings;

5. experience relatively less tension and anxiety because a part of themselves are not being denied; and

6. express their feelings in productive or neutral ways rather than being self-destructive or other-destructive.

When students can begin to apply their feelings to a learning situation, they then can be more creative. The facilitative teacher knows this and views feelings classes as an important way to free the intellect.

Feeling Class Activities
"Dear Abby" Discussion Groups

Purpose:

1. To identify and discuss personal problems that young people often encounter.

2. To recognize how feelings and behaviors are interrelated.

3. To develop and practice empathic skills.

4. To experience a problem-solving model that consists of identifying and exploring:

   a. feelings
   b. related behaviors
   c. possible consequences
   d. alternative solutions

Procedure:

1. Introduce the activity by bringing to class a newspaper that has a *Dear Abby* column. "Who recognizes this column in the paper?" "What can you tell me about *Dear Abby*?" As the students comment, listen and emphasize how the column is used, "to tell a problem and get advice," "to get something off your chest," "to see if anyone else has a problem like yours."

2. Read a question or problem from *Dear Abby*. "What do you suppose Abby would say?"

3. As soon as the students are motivated and seem to understand that people of all ages have problems and that many people seek understanding and help, distribute slips of paper and say, "Today we're going to begin our own version of *Dear Abby*. Start by writing down a question or problem that you have, or someone you know has, or that you think would be interesting to discuss. By the way, in talking with other students I have discovered some interesting problems that you might want to talk about, so I'll include a few of these."

Students do not sign their names and are told that each question or problem will be typed on another piece of paper and used for discussion at a later time. After the students have written their suggestions, the papers are collected. Here are some sample questions from elementary school cases:

Nobody likes me.
Others tease me because I'm dumb.
I have a bad temper that gets me in trouble.
Some boys chase me home after school and want to
   fight with me, and I don't know what to do.
I have to take care of my little sister all the time
   and can't play with others.
I want to play football but my mother won't let me. She
   treats me like a baby.

4. The class is divided into small discussion groups of five to six students. Each group is given two or three problems and members are given the task of responding to (a) how it would feel to have a problem like that, and (b) what do persons tend to do when they feel that way. Giving advice is not important at this time.

5. As soon as the groups have discussed the problems given to them, have the class form a semicircle. Each group is given an opportunity to relate its discussion experiences. As the discussions take place, continue to emphasize how feelings and behaviors are related, the consequences, behaviors, and possible alternatives. Remember, however, you are not Abby and your goal is to increase respect and understanding rather than to provide an answer or solution.

Discussion:
The following excerpts are taken from an eighth grade class's discussion following the *Dear Abby* activity.

Teacher:
(Begins by reading an anonymous statement from one of the slips of paper) "I have trouble saying 'no' when my friends offer me beer or cigarettes." Okay, how would you feel if you had a problem like that?

Female Student:
I've had a similar problem in the past, but I just decided one day that I would do what I wanted to do and not what my friends wanted me to do all the time.

Teacher:
You made a decision to do what you wanted to do (Clarification). But, what were you feeling in the situation (Open-ended question)?

Female Student:
Well, I guess I was feeling a lot of pressure from them to go along and I also felt put-off by it all.

Teacher:
You felt on the spot, at times, and it was unsettling to you (Feeling-focused).

Female Student:
Yeah, but it all worked out okay. They still like me.

Male Student:
I think sometimes that friends are just testing you, and that if they know you don't do stuff like that and then you give in to them, well, they'll be disappointed.

Teacher:
In other words, many times they don't really expect you to break your own rules (Clarification).

Male Student:
Yeah, it's like they're trying you a little bit.

Teacher:
Almost like testing you (Clarification).

Problem Moments: What Would You Do?

Purpose:
To learn how feelings are related to behaviors and to increase understanding.

Procedure:
1. Divide the class into small groups. Give each group a problem moment, such as the following:

   a. Jeff and Michele are making plans to go to a friend's party together the next night. Jeff told Michele he would call her at seven o'clock, but by nine o'clock he still had not called. What should she do?

   b. Joe and Sue are at a party. When the party is over, Sue doesn't want to go home. She wants to look for another party. Joe knows that her father and mother will be very angry if she does not arrive home, as agreed, and it's almost that time now. Joe thinks he is in love with Sue and wants to make her happy. What should Joe do?

   c. Jack likes Rosanna, but he is very shy and thinks that he is not a good dancer. He worries that it would be too embarrassing if she were to refuse him a date. He looks at the phone. What should he do?

   d. Mike and Diane are of different religious faiths. When Mike says at the dinner table that he would like to ask Diane to the senior prom, his parents raise questions and try to talk him out it. What should he do?

   e. Chuck's mother and father are separated. Chuck lives with his mother, who is resentful toward the father and does not want Chuck to visit him. Chuck wants very much to see his father but is very loyal to his mother. They talk at the dinner table. What should he say?

   f. Martha, who has always gone to church with her mother, has gradually lost her faith in the church and had decided that it is hypocritical for her to attend church. Talking it over with her friend, Martha says, "Should I attend church anyway and not let my mother know how I feel?

   g. Ted and his father do not get along. Ted wants to enlist in the armed forces, just to get away from the family. His mother wants him stay at home and go to a local college. Late one night he is talking the situation over with his friend. If you were that friend, what would you say or do?

2. Each group discusses what they would do in these situations and arrives at a certain way of acting out the solution for the rest of the class.

3. The solution is role-played.

4. Lead the class in a discussion with the same focus as other feelings classes (See the *Dear Abby* activity). Avoid rushing in with advice; rather focus on what people are experiencing or feeling, and what those feelings might make a person want to do. What information is missing? Would that make a difference in what might be done to be helpful? How can you help people when they have problems?

5. Replay some of the endings with changes suggested by the class.

Pantomiming Emotions

Purpose:

To recognize feelings and to understand how body movements reflect feelings.

Procedure:

1. Ask a student to select some emotion—a pleasant or unpleasant feeling—previously felt and have the student try to communicate that emotion to the group through pantomime. Then, have the student pantomime a contrasting emotion.

2. The teacher can make the pantomime procedure a game by keeping the emotion a secret. Whisper the word into the ear of the person who is to pantomime the feeling and then the class has to guess the feeling after the person has pantomimed it for 10-15 seconds.

3. Or, a group of students could be given a list of emotions to pantomime as a group. The group discusses what behaviors should be demonstrated in order to help the class guess the emotion. Perhaps an incident that portrays a strong feeling might be developed by the group. In this case, the group acts out the situation fully before the class tries to guess the emotion being portrayed. The class then talks about those behaviors that were clues to the emotion.

Other Feelings Classes Procedures
Feelings Tally

Procedure:

Ask students to write down, in one minute's time, as many emotions or feelings that they can recall. The total number of feelings each student writes down can be tallied. The class can discuss its reactions as to why some members wrote many feelings while other members wrote only a few.

Then ask members to compare the pleasant and unpleasant feeling word tallies and discuss their reactions. The most frequent feelings are love, hate, anger, and fear. Students tend to list more unpleasant feeling words than positive ones. What might account for this? Discuss why a few words appear on the lists more than others. Discuss which of the feelings are comfortable to them, uncomfortable, and how these feelings are expressed in their lives.

Group Pictures

Procedure:

Provide the class with a set of pictures or cartoons depicting groups: meetings, families, couples, children, and so forth. Each person in the group selects a picture to which one is positively drawn and tells a story about it; then the least attractive picture might be selected and a story is told. Or, the selection of a picture can be based on other variables such as a memory, a wish, a reflection of oneself, a goal.

Unfair Debate

Procedure:
Ask two or three students to volunteer for an experiment in group interaction. The volunteers are asked to leave the room. While they are gone, tell the class that when the two or three return, others will engage them in an argument at the first opportunity. The point is to argue as unfairly as possible, interrupting, introducing irrelevancies, contradicting themselves, becoming over-excited, inventing facts, and pointing out non-existent fallacies. The rest of the group is asked to be as observant as possible about the reactions of the volunteers to this unfair interaction. The volunteers are asked to return and the meeting proceeds. The debate is carried out as long as it is feasible to elicit feelings and behaviors before a class discussion begins about what was seen and heard.

Feelings and Music

Procedure:
Select a few records to play which feature contrasting sounds (e.g., dreamy, soft music vs. lively, spirited jazz). Students draw a picture according to the sound of the music, getting into the feeling(s) that the music gives them. The picture may show a scene in one's life or be an abstract. Pictures are then shown to the class and discussed. A variation of this procedure is to have students act out individually, or as a group, a situation suggested to them by the music.

Sociodrama

Procedure:

Select a problem in human relationships that fits the maturity level of your students. You may find a short story that serves the purpose and which can be read to the class. You may, however, write your own story or simply describe the characters and the situation in which they are involved. Or, you might ask your students to write stories to be used in the class. In any event, the number of characters should be limited and several different endings should be possible.

Before you or a student reads the story, prepare the students to identify with the characters by explaining that you may choose some class members to act out the ending of the story that they are about to hear. Then, read or tell the story, which takes no longer than five minutes.

Either choose the cast or ask for volunteers. For your first sociodrama, you might choose boys and girls who will cooperate and be able to talk readily. After you have used the technique a number of times, you could then chose stories and select students who would gain the most from playing the roles. For example, when you know a boy has no appreciation for the job of a teacher, cast him in the role of a teacher.

The cast might be sent out of the room for a three-to five-minute planning session. While the play is in progress, do not interrupt the players. You should, however, recognize when enough information has been presented, perhaps a decision has been reached, and help end the scene if necessary.

Have the class evaluate the scene in terms of (a) emotional reactions portrayed; (b) facts cited; and, (c) consequences of the actions. Do not evaluate students' emotional reactions and beware of amateur psychological diagnosis on the part of students. They were only playing roles.

Inside-Outside Circle

Procedure:

This procedure has sometimes been referred to as the "fishbowl." Two circles are formed, one within the other. Members on the inside circle are given a task, while members of the outside circle remain silent and observe. The outsider members are later asked to give feedback to individual members of the group or the group as a whole. Later the roles are reversed.

Go-Around

Procedure:

Go-Around is a procedure that directs each member of a small group to participate in turn. It is a procedure that encourages each member to respond to a task and provides equal opportunity for all members of a group to be involved. For example, following a particular presentation by a teacher, or perhaps following a certain activity, students are asked to write down two feeling words that describe how they are feeling now that the activity is completed. Then in a Go-Around, each student tells the rest of the group the words written down. No attempt is made to discuss the feelings at that moment. After everyone has revealed the feeling words, the group can continue with the activity or focus on the experience and material that was elicited from the Go-Around.

Go-Around tasks might be: Tell about a job you would like to have someday; Tell about a time when you felt successful; Tell about something you would change about yourself; Tell about a change you'd make at school to make it a better place for you; Tell who you most admire; Tell about a famous person you'd like to interview; Tell about a time when you felt shy; Tell about a time when you were proud of something; Tell what you like best about this school or class.

Section Three:

Communication

A large portion of our lives is spent trying to communicate with others in one fashion or another. Human problems are often the result of a communication breakdown and many people seek professional counseling or therapy because of interpersonal conflicts.

Each of us has a unique perceptual field. True communication with another is the function of merging two perceptual fields. The two fields must overlap if two-way communication is to occur. When an overlap in perceptual fields occurs, we have accurate understanding and positive identification.

When we think of communication we tend to think of people talking to each other. We think of spoken or written words. They help to transmit meaning and the ability to use them makes us effective communicators.

Communication also occurs at a nonverbal level. Body language is just as important as the words that are used to convey a thought. Our face is one part of our body that reveals feelings. Our eyes, for example, can say many things. They can communicate a warm welcome or an icy attitude. They can invite people to talk more or dismiss them with a disinterested glance.

In this section there are several activities, both verbal and nonverbal, that will aid in the development of communication skills.

Verbal Communication Procedures
Learning to be Facilitative

Purpose:

The purpose of this activity is to learn and practice the facilitative responses (Feeling-focused; Clarifying and Summarizing responses) as presented in Chapter 3. It will also increase two-way communication among students.

Procedure:

1. Reread Chapter 3 regarding the high facilitative responses and discuss them with your class.

2. Divide the class into triads. Ask students to join with people that they know the least. Have members of the triad number off 1, 2, and 3. Let No. 1 be the talker, No. 2 the facilitator, and No. 3 the observer.

3. The talker speaks to the facilitator for three minutes regarding one's negative feelings about the class. (Other "talker" assignments could be: What you like least about school. Or, something about yourself that gets in the way of being a better student or working better with your teachers.)

   The facilitator should make only high facilitative responses, thus assisting the talker to share ideas and feelings. This is not a time to agree, show disapproval, or give advice. The task is to be a facilitative listener.

4. During the three minutes the observer watches the facilitator and records observations by making out The Facilitator's Report Card. Later, the observer will give feedback to the facilitator.

5. After three minutes, the observer, using The Facilitator's Report Card, feeds back the observations to the facilitator for about two minutes.

6. Next, give the talker a new assignment. The talker should speak for about another three minutes on the positive aspects of the class (or school, or self). The assignments for the other two in the triad remain the same. Time is taken for feedback again.

7. Then, roles are switched in a second and third round (with the same talking assignments) until all three persons have been in each role.

The Facilitator's Report Card

	Strongly Agree				Strongly Disagree
	1	2	3	4	5

The listener:

1. Interpreted or analyzed   ☐ ☐ ☐ ☐ ☐

2. Evaluated or gave advice   ☐ ☐ ☐ ☐ ☐

3. Used open-ended questions   ☐ ☐ ☐ ☐ ☐

4. Responded to feelings   ☐ ☐ ☐ ☐ ☐

5. Listened well   ☐ ☐ ☐ ☐ ☐

6. Supported and reassured   ☐ ☐ ☐ ☐ ☐

7. Interrupted unnecessarily   ☐ ☐ ☐ ☐ ☐

8. Attempted to clarify by using fresh words   ☐ ☐ ☐ ☐ ☐

9. Seemed interested in what the talker was saying   ☐ ☐ ☐ ☐ ☐

10. Facilitated the talker to continue talking   ☐ ☐ ☐ ☐ ☐

11. Denied or avoided obvious feelings of the talker   ☐ ☐ ☐ ☐ ☐

12. Had good eye contact   ☐ ☐ ☐ ☐ ☐

Discussion:

Most of the people (both adults and children) who have experienced this activity have indicated that they felt awkward and self-conscious at first. This is not everyday conversation and the experience may elicit feelings of self-consciousness. The facilitators may feel mechanical, but they should not let this hinder their practice of the facilitative skills. Only through practice will the unpleasant feelings lessen and self-confidence grow.

This activity takes approximately one-half hour, although time can be increased. You could use additional time for discussion before starting each round. Students will have questions about the use of the facilitative responses. Encourage them to look for opportunities to respond to feelings and to avoid asking too many questions. Some students may learn that if they can ask a question, they can recast their words and make a clarifying or feeling-focused statement (Chapter 3).

Each time, before the observer gives feedback to the facilitator, you might make statements such as:

> *Now, observer, tell the facilitator about what you saw and heard. Was the person sensitive? Was the person a good listener? Did the facilitator have good eye contact? Did the facilitator reflect and clarify without giving approval or disapproval? Okay. Talk to the facilitator for about two minutes while the talker just listens and watches without comment.*

You will notice that by the time you get to the third talker (third round), you will have a more difficult time getting the triads to stop their interactions. The noise level will increase progressively during this activity. As students come to know and trust each other better, they want to share more of their thoughts and feelings. Nobody is on the spot for too long—three minutes—and it is usually an enjoyable experience to receive personal attention for that long.

Some students might ask how to facilitate someone who is shy and quiet. As humans we cannot not communicate. Thus, they should put themselves in the other person's place and sense how the world appears to that person at that moment, perhaps clarifying or focusing on a feeling that the person might be experiencing. Ask the students to be aware of whatever they see and hear, and to say something in a facilitative manner.

The procedures used in this triad activity can also be used in academic areas by simply changing the talker's assignment (e.g. talk about a particular assignment, what the talker would say to a famous person in history, hidden messages in favorite commercials, community or state political issues, the most confusing and interesting part of a short story, good and poor study habits). The report card can also be tailored to fit special objectives.

One and Two-Way Communication

Purpose:

To be aware of how communication between people can be one-way or two-way and the impact on a given task.

Procedure:

1. Begin the class with a discussion of one-and two-way communication. A lecture, written instructions for a test, and memo are familiar examples of one-way communication. A teacher lecturing with one's back to the students while writing on the board during announcements over the public address system is one example.

2. Prior to the activity, on separate pieces of paper, copy each of the three drawings in Figure 1.

Figure 1

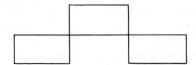

Figure 1(a)

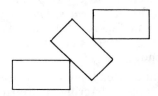

Figure 1(b)

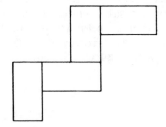

Figure 1(c)

3. Choose a class member to be the sender. Each student should have a paper and a pencil and be prepared to follow the sender's directions. Hide the sender from view. (Or take precautions to have the sender carefully avoid giving clues to the group.) Give the sender three minutes to describe Figure 1(a), using any directions desired, in an effort to help the rest of the class draw the figure on their papers. This is one-way communication and there can be no eye contact or questions from the receivers.

NOTE: Confusion usually exists at this time and you may want to bring this out in the discussion later. Take note of their behaviors. How did they react when it became confusing?

4. When the three minutes are up, ask the receivers to write one word on their papers that best describes their feelings at that moment.

5. Let the sender show Figure 1(a) to the receivers and then lead a class discussion with a focus on feelings. Unless the sender or receivers are exceptional, very few students will have an accurate drawing. Ask them to discuss how the absence of eye contact affected them, what the notion of "no questions" did to them, and so forth. How did the sender feel?

6. Begin a second round by choosing a new sender; give the sender Figure 1(b) and repeat the above procedures. However, the receivers, as a group, may ask five questions during this three minutes. You will notice that this drawing is more difficult than Figure 1(a). However, because of the two-way interaction, more students will draw it accurately. Discuss the round.

7. Select a different sender for the third round and give that person three minutes to describe Figure 1(c). Do not hide the sender and allow as much interaction as possible between the sender and the receivers. Although this drawing is more difficult to describe, greater accuracy in the receivers' drawings will generally result. Senders might be more frustrated with Figure 1(c) than with Figure 1(a) in that two-way communication takes longer. However, the receivers usually feel more confident with Figures 1(b) and 1(c) than with Figure 1(a).

200 Years from Now

Purpose:

To enhance communication among students regarding their values and choices. Materials for this activity might include pictorial magazines, scissors, and colored construction paper.

Procedure:

1. Divide the class into groups of about five or six and appoint a recording secretary for each one. The task for each group is to put together a time capsule that will fully describe their particular group to people who will be living 200 years from now.

2. Tell each group that they must decide on:

   a. four musical recordings
   b. five magazine pictures
   c. an original paragraph, poem, or short story
   d. four significant events of the past five years that depict them today and will best describe their particular group to people who will be living 200 years from now.

The five magazine pictures could be pasted or taped to a piece of construction paper. After each group has decided on its four recordings, its pictures, and the historical events, it should add anything else to its time capsule that the respective group members would like to add. Then, in turn, have the recording secretaries report and show the class the time capsules.

3. Ask the class, as a whole group, to decide on one capsule to represent the class.

Pick Your Corner

Purpose:

To stimulate communication on important issues, to force and clarify positions, and to increase understanding of other's points of view.

Procedure:

1. Designate one corner of the room as the "Strongly Disagree" section, another as the "Strongly Agree" section, another as "Disagree," and the fourth as "Agree." The center of the room might be designated as "Uncertain." Then, make a statement such as the following: Our country treats criminals honestly and fairly.

2. Give the students a moment to think about the five options in the five sections of the room. Then, on a given signal, they are to go the corner that matches their personal opinions.

3. Allow time for the participants in each corner to discuss among themselves their reasons for choosing the particular corner. They might even make a list of reasons that led them to be there.

4. Hold a general class discussion, as members listen to the statements by each of the sections.

5. You might bring the "Strongly Agree" corner into a meeting with the "Strongly Disagree", perhaps debating the issue or trying to convince the "Uncertain" or undecided group what to do.

6. You might reassemble the class. Read the statement again and ask the students to go to the corner their parents (or teachers) would choose. Again, allow time for discussion among those students who selected a particular corner.

Other statements might include the following:

My country, right or wrong, but my country!

Children should have the right to choose their own dress code, at home and at school.

People who cheat on tests will cheat in other situations too.

Corporal punishment is effective for changing student behavior.

Peer pressure is a myth because everyone makes their own choices.

The legal age for getting a driver's license should be 20.

Every student should be paid a stipend (allowance) for going to school, with the best academic students getting the most money.

The statements should be appropriate for the grade level of your students and they should be issues that are timely and thought provoking.

Communication Between the Sexes

Purpose:
To facilitate communication between boys and girls, to heighten awareness of sex role stereotypes.

Procedure:
1. Form two circles, one circle within another. Girls sit in the inside circle while boys sit on the outside.

2. For the first ten minutes the girls are encouraged to talk about boys, venting their unpleasant and pleasant feelings. What are their pet peeves? How do they think boys see girls? The outer circle (males) observes but does not participate.

3. After about ten minutes, the circles are reversed, with the males on the inside responding to the same questions and tasks.

4. Both groups together then discuss how they felt about the activity and what they learned from it. Additional questions to each group might be posed by group members or the teacher.

Variations:
a. Females sit in the inside circle and pretend they are males. They talk about how it feels to be "male" and what they like and dislike about it. They might also talk about how they see females, or talk about "things I like and dislike about being a girl or boy," or "things that I would like to change in our society in terms of being masculine or feminine." Each group might be encouraged to talk about the biggest problem of the opposite sex.

b. The males write statements about what it feels like to be a boy and some of their likes and dislikes. The statements are then given to the circle of females, who read them and respond. For example, "My girl makes me feel cheap when I can't afford to take her to some places," or, "Why do boys always have to be the ones to set up a date?" or "I like a girl, but she doesn't like me."

Other Verbal Communication Procedures

Focusing on Feelings

Procedure:
Divide participants into dyads. One partner talks for two to three minutes on any topic of concern, while the other partner listens. When the first talker finishes, the other members tells in two minutes or less what feelings were perceived—the feelings behind the statements. Then, the partners exchange roles and repeat the procedure.

Thank You Cards

Procedure:
This is similar to the above procedure, except group members share their perceptions. Have each member of a small group give a three- or four-minute presentation on a topic of concern. Following each presentation, other members of the group are allowed to reflect on the feelings behind the presentation. As soon as all members have presented and reacted, give one card to each member of the group with these words typed on it: "Thank you for listening and understanding me." Then have each member give the card to the member of the group who is perceived as most deserving of it.

Three Significant People

Procedure:
Give the class the following instructions:

List the names of three important persons who you will probably communicate with during the next week. For each person, briefly describe how you think that person sees the world. How does each vision of the world differ from yours? How is it the same? If you were asked to say three things about each of these persons, what would you say? What have these people done in your life that makes them important or significant to you? What roles do they play in your life? What roles do you expect them to play? What roles do they expect from you?

The class is divided into small groups for discussion purposes.

Gossip Game

Procedure:
Set up an experiment with six or more persons. Select a rather short story or anecdote. Have five of the six persons leave the room. Tell the story to the one remaining and then bring in a second person from outside. Have the one to whom you tell it to the third person and so on. Have the rest of the class (as observers) identify the precise points where variation takes place. How is this "gossip game" related to the kinds of communication that often take place in the real world of gossips?

A Triadic Interview

Procedure:
Divide the class into groups of three, number off, and have each group conduct a triadic interview.

1. Number one will be interviewed privately by number two. The purpose of the interview is to find out as much as possible about number one.

2. Number two will be interviewed by number three to find out what number two discovered about number one, who must be present at this second interview but cannot participate until the interview is over. At that time, number one may correct misinformation or misunderstandings and give one's reactions to what was selected for communication.

What factors led to any misinformation or misunderstandings? What left out information would number one want number two to have included? What information did number three want, but it was not available from number two? Did this experience help the three people to understand each other better? All three persons can play all three parts.

The Alter-Ego and Role-Reversal

Procedure:
Have one person stand behind another who is talking and try to put oneself mentally in the place of the other. Periodically that person should state how one thinks the other feels. Or, sometimes have the people reverse roles, acting the behaviors and attempting to see how it feels to be the other person. Have them exchange seats and assume the other's posture, language, and so forth.

Rituals

Procedure:
Divide the class into groups and ask each one to create a new social ritual. A ritual can be developed to replace one that already exists or a completely new ritual can be designed. The class reassembles and each group demonstrates the new ritual. The whole class might be led through the new ritual.

The Gibberish Game

Procedure:
Form small groups of perhaps four to five persons each. A series of gibberish games is begun by first demonstrating gibberish (nonsense syllables). The groups are then instructed to converse using only gibberish. After a few minutes, or on a signal, each group is asked to slowly and gradually begin to exclude one of the people from the conversation, without deciding ahead of time who that person will be and without using any signs or signals. The participants are instructed to be aware of whether they are "in" or whether they are being excluded and to be aware of how they feel in the position.

Gibberish might also be used to experience the phenomenon of name calling. In this case, individuals are assigned a gibberish name that has no meaning but can be experienced as either positive or negative. Participants practice saying the gibberish term with different voice inflections and intonations.

Dialogue Chair

Procedure:
Two empty chairs are placed in the middle of the circle. A group member sits in one chair and faces the empty chair and tells the group who is in the other chair. The speaker carries on a dialogue with the empty chair, perhaps what one would like to say to the missing person. The speaker then sits in the empty chair, responding and talking as one believes the other person would in responding.

Poor Communication

Procedure:
Ask your class to think over the events of the past week. How many instances can they recall of poor communication? Have them write a brief summary of one such incident, describing the situation and consequences. Divide the class into groups and have them identify common themes from the incidents.

Group Roles

Procedure:
Divide the class into small groups. Each group is asked to discuss various roles that are often played by individuals when they are in a group. For example, initiator, blocker, dominator, withdrawn person, supporter, challenger, negative attitude, and so forth. After about 15 minutes, each individual writes down the adjectives, verbs, and descriptive phrases that most typically describe the roles played by the members in the group.

Sometimes the groups will take a brief rest and then reassemble. They are then given a second task. Each member looks at the descriptors and then writes words that describe oneself. Since these words describe one's typical role in a group, the next period of time (perhaps 15 minutes) is used to allow each individual to behave in just the opposite way. You might say:

> *As you look at the words in front of you (for easy reference), try experimenting with some verbal and non-verbal behaviors that are not typical of yourself in a group. This is not an easy task, but do not be discouraged. Keep the group moving on the discussion topic as you try out your "new" role.*

The procedure can produce tension, confusion, and laughter. It allows people to try out and practice new behaviors. Some feel excited while others may feel guilty. Some feel free while others feel restricted. Some might feel a sense of release from an inhibiting role while others are more tense.

Symbolic Hats

Procedure:
Using hats that describe various occupational roles—policemen, soldier, fireman, farmer—or other roles such as teacher, principal, or parent. Have the students, usually beginning with two at a time, play out a scene in which the roles that these hats symbolize are portrayed.

Nonverbal Communication Procedures

There are many things that can be done in your class that would be classified as nonverbal communication procedures. Here are some that might be used.

Ask your students to:

1. Observe another person and take note of the nonverbal messages that person tends to send. Observe carefully and write down the messages sent by others, such as teachers or parents through nonverbal behavior. (You may want your students to do this regarding your own nonverbal communication. If you plan to collect the papers when they describe you, have the students remain anonymous.)

2. Improvise a story without words. Role playing can be used for charades or pantomime.

3. Sit face to face with a friend and let your eyes speak to each other with no verbalizing. What messages can you give and receive? Some have said that the eyes are the mirror of the soul. What has your experience in this case done to make you agree or disagree with this statement?

4. Select words from a list of emotions and have students choose some that seem difficult for them to express and to try to express them nonverbally to someone else or to a group through pantomime. Possible emotions to use include fear, security, hate, love, approval, rejection, sureness, anxiety, exhilaration, success or failure.

5. Use a tom-tom, a small drum, or a set of drums to beat out a rhythm that conveys a message to another person in the group. Try to make the message as specific as possible without using words or gestures.

6. Use musical instruments to find a rhythm or beat that feels good to them. Each is to beat out the rhythm until one becomes satisfied with it. Next, the student is to find another person and share the rhythm or beat. Let both get involved in the sharing. After a period of time in which they have listened to each others rhythm and beat, ask them to put the two together. This activity may also be done with a group where all members put their beats together.

After any of these procedures, you might ask, "What did you experience when you did this activity? What were some of your feelings? Okay, what were some of your thoughts as you were going through the activity?" Encourage students to discuss their pleasant and unpleasant feelings. Model the high facilitative responses as you lead the discussions.

Expressing Emotions Nonverbally

Procedure:

This is a nonverbal activity in which class members are asked to express various emotions.

1. Divide the class into pairs.

2. Give one member of each dyad a card on which is written an emotion (e.g., anger, trust, love, fear, hate, sympathy, or tenderness). This person attempts to express the emotion in a nonverbal manner. The other person is to guess the emotion. Only one emotion is given at a time and each of the dyads can take turns or can work with different emotions.

3. When the exercise is completed, have the dyads return to a group, approximately ten minutes, and discuss the experience. What part of the body was most effective in communicating a particular emotion? How accurate was the receiver in guessing the emotion? Did the member of the dyad who was communicating the emotion feel it? If so, where? How were the hands, eyes, mouth, and body stance used in the transmission?

4. Variations: Use paper masks. Do the same exercise but this time have all the facial expressions obscured. Thus, only the body is available to communicate the emotions. Members can become aware of body movements that are used in nonverbal communication. They may realize how little (how much) they use their bodies to communicate.

Mirroring

Procedure:

Form dyads. One of the pair becomes a mirror, the other becomes the communicator. The mirror cannot talk, but it reflects everything it sees. The communicator, by observing one's reflections in the mirror, can get feedback about oneself. The mirror, by reflecting what it sees, can get in touch with the person being reflected.

Roles are reversed after about five minutes. After five more minutes, the dyads are given the opportunity to talk about what they have experienced. Finally, participants are instructed to become both mirror and communicator at the same time and to create a dialogue of movement with their partners. After about 5 minutes, the group is called together into a circle for discussion.

Finding a Group

Procedure:
Have students mill about in the center of the room and, without talking, end up in groups of exactly four people. If there are five, one has to leave. If there are three, someone has to be found to join this group. Discuss the process through which the groups were formed and what caused the students to choose the group they chose.

Cooperation Game

Procedure:
Teams of five people each work together, without talking, to solve a puzzle problem. Each team is given five pieces of paper that do not form a square. Their task is to get from other team members the necessary pieces they will need in order to complete a square. If you add an element of competition—that is, the first team to complete its square wins—you may find that some rules are helpful. Team members cannot get a piece until they give one away, thereby assuring that each team always has five pieces.

Feeling Space

Procedure:
Divide the class into small groups. Ask members of the groups to stand, close their eyes, stretch out their hands and become aware of their contact with others. This exercise should last for about five minutes. Discussion afterward can introduce the topic of aloneness and feelings about contact.

Back to Back

Procedure:
This is a three-part exercise in communication using dyads. First, sitting back-to-back, individuals communicate to one another by talking, but without turning their heads. Since all of the dyads in a group are talking at once and since talk is primarily without the nonverbal cues that are used for understanding, this can be a frustrating experience. Individuals are supposed to experience the frustration.

After five minutes the partners are asked to turn their chairs around and face one another. They are then to communicate by only using their eyes. They are told to get in touch with how they feel as they do this; if they want to look away, that is okay as long as they are aware of the feelings they are having.

After a few moments they sit back and close their eyes and "see what is going on with you now." Do you have some ideas about your new friend? Now, put these aside and open your eyes and see if you can view your friend as if you were seeing that person for the first time.

The third part of the exercise involves closing the eyes and communicating only by touching hands. They can communicate in any way they wish. In our Western culture the risk of touching except in routine, socially acceptable ways, such as shaking hands or patting someone on the back, can be a problem in communication. In a group situation, the risk is somewhat diminished, as everyone is involved in the activity. At first, however, the same kinds of feelings that cause us to be reserved in our touching of others will likely be present.

Hand Communication

Purpose:
Ask your class members to select a partner from the class among those they know least well. These two should then stand face to face with eyes closed, touch hands, and not talk to each other. Ask them to send a message or to respond to their partner through use of their hands.

Then, give instructions similar to these:

> *Now, describe to your partner what you meant by your hand communication. Listen to what your partner tried to communicate to you. How close did you come to communicating with each other? Were there things your hands said to your partner that you could not have put into words? If you were to talk again, using only your hands, would you now be more effective since you have now verbalized some of your thoughts?*

Initially, you and your students may feel awkward when you use these nonverbal activities involving emotions. To share emotions at all is difficult for some students; to do so nonverbally makes the task even harder. But if the classroom atmosphere is one of warmth and trust, and if open, facilitative discussions can occur, then a breaking down of many barriers to communication will soon begin.

The Rope Game

Purpose:
Divide the class into groups of 8 or 10 and supply each group with a large knotted rope. Indicate that they may do anything they choose with the rope but there is to be no talking. The group is then left alone and given the freedom to work with the rope.

After a few minutes of silence the group will usually begin milling around and thinking of different ways the rope may be used. You may designate observers on the outside to count the number of ways the group discovered to use the rope. They can also watch to see if the behavior in the group is related to behavior in everyday life. For example, are the members of the group cooperative, hesitant, hostile, and so forth. How much resistance existed at the beginning and how much at the end? Was the behavior at the beginning the same as at the end?

Section Four:

Self-Awareness and Self-Disclosure

☐ **The Self-Disclosing Flag**   ☐ **Who Am I?**
☐ **Name Collage**   ☐ **Heroes**
☐ **The Here and Now**   ☐ **Your Most Important Beliefs**
☐ **The Self-Disclosing Scroll**   ☐ **Draw Yourself**
☐ **Aimlessness**   ☐ **Symbolic Objects**
☐ **Feeling Cards**   ☐ **Birth Order**
☐ **Ups and Downs**   ☐ **Grocery Bag**
☐ **Developing the Senses**   ☐ **Clothes with a Meaning**

Self-Awareness

Self-awareness is a concept that has become increasingly popular over the years. Most of us assume that we know a great deal about ourselves. We know where we were born, the schools we have attended, satisfying and disappointing events in our lives, people we respect, and a host of other things, including a general idea of things in the future that we hope will happen to us.

For the most part, we are in touch with the basic factors about ourselves. But, sometimes the basic facts cover up our real selves and serve as a facade. In a sense, events may have no meaning without feelings. People are interested in our reactions to events, perhaps more so than the actual events themselves.

Knowledge of ourselves, then, is more than our just being aware of significant happenings in our lives. It is being aware of the "me" and the impact that things have on the "me." Do you have a complete picture of yourself? If someone were to say, "Tell me about yourself," where would you begin?

The process of becoming self-aware means acknowledging those factors that tend to influence our lives. That is, factors that cannot only be documented by history, but those that are ongoing and which combine to create our unique life styles. Being aware of self means knowing our feelings, special needs, goals, and typical behaviors. If we are to become more aware of ourselves, we must know about significant people who we admire and who have influenced our lives, ideas that tend to captivate our imagination, and values that seem to influence most of our decisions.

Theoretically, to be totally aware of one's self might be an impossible task. The self is generally resistant to change, yet it is always changing, moving toward some other potential. The process of attempting self-realization can prove to be valuable. Self-awareness involves a self-inventory, a bit of introspection, some self-analysis, and so forth. However, it is doubtful that a person can gain self-awareness without the help of someone else. Self-disclosure in the presence of others assists us to understand ourselves better.

Increased self-awareness can come about through trying new experiences and taking note of our reactions, feelings, conflicts, and general impressions. Even repeating old and regular experiences, but taking careful note of pleasures and dissatisfactions that may accompany the experiences, can prove valuable. It is a process of tuning in on where and who we are in a situation and facing the truth about ourselves. It involves a stripping away of the rationalization and other defenses that often prevent us from being in touch with a deeper level of ourselves, particularly our feeling selves.

Self-Disclosure

We cannot *not* communicate. We communicate something of ourselves to others all the time. From our actions they form impressions about us and eventually form a picture of us. They use that picture, constructed from the perceptions of our behaviors, as a guideline to relate to us. For example, if people see you as an individual who enjoys arguing, they may bait you, or maybe avoid bringing up certain subjects because they believe that you will be argumentative. Perhaps through your self-disclosure, people can know and understand you better.

Self-disclosure is a conscious self-revelation process. It is willingly and purposefully telling another what you are thinking and feeling. It may deal with something past or it may focus on your immediate feelings and ideas. Self-disclosure is essential if close personal relationships are to be formed.

For example, if an individual were to describe Disney World to you, but leave out their impressions and feelings, you would more than likely find the conversation a bit dull and drab. When people put themselves, their feelings, and special impressions into a situation, they disclose a special part of themselves with which you can identify. Although we may all have experienced some of the same events in our lives, it is the feelings about those events that give us our common bond.

This particular concept can be helpful to us when we are working with persons of another generation, sex, or race. That is, while we may never have experienced the same critical events that a person relates to us, it is possible for us to identify with the feelings experienced during those events. People who relate embarrassing moments in their lives can strike an understanding and sympathetic part of us which brings us closer to them.

What determines whether or not we will disclose a part of ourselves to others? As you know, we all tend to be selective in what we disclose to others. Most often, we will not disclose ourselves to others if we feel that it will threaten our survival, either the physical or psychological self. Self-disclosure involves an element of risk. It suggests that we are willing to trust others not to use what we tell them to cause us hurt or pain.

Self-disclosure and self-awareness help us realize more of ourselves and our potential. Self-awareness increases self acceptance and as we accept ourselves more, we tend to feel greater responsibility for ourselves. We feel more in control and experience less defensiveness and tension.

The process of self-awareness enables us to tune into ourselves and identify those parts that prevent us from being fully-functioning. Obviously, increased self-awareness then can lead to increased self-confidence. It also leads to clearer understanding of our goals and the ways in which we seek to meet our needs. Students cannot grow personally and academically in a classroom unless the processes of self-disclosure and self-awareness are an integral part of the learning environment.

The facilitative teacher recognizes that one of the fundamental tasks of structuring a learning experience is to help students to become involved in the learning process, to see how the experience is related to them, to take it into their personal awareness, and then to disclose to others their experiences. The facilitative responses (Chapter 3) have been viewed in terms of the probability that they can assist an individual, or a group of persons, become more self-disclosing and self-aware.

Sometimes facilitative activities such as the following can provide a valuable learning experience. While any of the activities may be used separately, they have special relevance when they are incorporated into the regular school curriculum as part of a learning unit.

Self-Awareness and
Self-Disclosure Activities

The Self-Disclosing Flag

Purpose:
The purpose of this activity is to help students to self-disclose about themselves and to help others become better acquainted with them. The structure provides a similar disclosing area for each participant, thus producing a reassuring and identity building kind of experience.

Procedure:
1. Ask each class member to draw a flag covering most of a piece of 8 1/2 by 11 inch unlined paper. Each one then divides the flag into six parts, beginning with one vertical line down the middle and two horizontal lines drawn equally apart on the flag. As soon as all members have drawn and divided their flags, lead them through each area by giving the following directions:

2. Directions:
   a. In the upper left hand corner draw a symbol that you think best depicts this class. (Members should be given ample time to draw a symbol, but the emphasis is not on their artwork. The symbol only needs to have meaning to them at this point.)

   b. In the upper right hand corner draw a symbol that represents a time when you had an unpleasant experience in school.

   c. In the left hand middle area draw a symbol depicting a time when you had a pleasant experience in school.

   d. In the right hand middle area draw a symbol representing something in which you someday would like to be successful.

   e. In the lower left hand area draw a symbol that represents something about yourself that you will have to overcome before being successful.

   f. In the lower right hand corner list three adjectives that you feel the teacher in this class would use to describe you.

3. Divide the class into small groups. You may use the results in several ways:

   a. One member may begin and discuss each symbol in the flag.

   b. One member may discuss an area that can be shared with the other members of the group. Following the discussion, another person shares a particular symbol of one's own choice.

   c. In a go-around process, a member may share one symbol and tell about it. Or, that person might share which one was the easiest to think about and the one that was the most difficult to think about.

   d. You may ask that all flags be exposed in front of the group and that one member select one that is interesting or appealing and asks for more information.

   e. After each member has shared one or two symbols, a member might be given an opportunity to look around the group and request more information regarding a particular symbol.

4. It is not necessary that a person be pressed to reveal everything put on the flag. It should also be emphasized that the flag could well change within another time period, for example, within one or two days or within the next half hour. Moreover, a person may have decided to select one of several choices to reveal on the flag. This may lead to a discussion of why the member selected that symbol to reveal to the group and why others were omitted. Several students have indicated after the experience that they wanted an opportunity to change a symbol. There may be some members who risk something of themselves, yet do not feel comfortable sharing it with the group. In general, it is best for students to volunteer to share what they have drawn.

5. After the initial self-disclosing process, you might encourage all members to look for common themes that seem to run through the shared symbols.

More Variations

The self-disclosing flag is only a vehicle to promote the process of self-disclosure. It should not become an end in itself. The directions for using symbols may be altered for various groups. For example, you might ask students to list in various parts of the flag the following:

- The most embarrassing moment in one's life.
- The most important belief about oneself.
- Something that might be expected to happen to a person within the next five years.
- The most or the least liked experience.
- A favorite or least favorite television program.
- School subjects most and least liked.
- A unique part of oneself that can be a sustaining force through life.

The Here and Now

Purpose:

To increase awareness of self in the here and now, to encourage self-disclosure, and to provide personal feedback.

Procedure:

1. Divide the class into small groups of 6-7.

2. Moving around the circle one at a time, each person talks in a "stream of consciousness," getting into an "awareness" of oneself. Both physical sensations and mental feelings can be reviewed.

3. The following rules are observed:

    a. Each "awareness" must be a self-awareness. That is, the student must share something of one's self rather than focusing on someone else.

    b. Each awareness must be a "here and now" awareness. For example, "I am aware I am feeling anxious."

    c. Each new awareness must be spoken by beginning with the phrase, "I am aware of...." For example, "I am aware I am sitting here." "I am aware I am the focus of attention." "I am aware I should be saying something." "I am aware I am becoming more relaxed."

    d. "Owning" or responsibility must be assumed for each awareness through the language used in speaking about it. For example, "I am aware that I am clenching my fist." Or, "I am aware that my fist is clenched." This particular concept is more difficult, but it does emphasize the personal responsibility of awareness and sensation.

    e. Sometimes it might be appropriate to say, "I am aware of my looking into your eyes; I am aware of my not wanting to tell you what I'm feeling and thinking right now."

    f. Censoring is permissible. A group member might say, "I am aware of looking at Fred. I am aware of his blue eyes. I am aware of not wanting to say any more."

    g. Members stop when they say, "I am aware of wanting to stop. I am aware of stopping. I am going to stop. I have stopped." The next person then proceeds in a "go-around" procedure.

h. Anyone who does not want to participate should be encouraged to say, "I am aware of not wanting to do this. I am aware of refusing. I refuse to do this."

4. After the last person has finished, the group discusses how they felt during the procedure, both about themselves and about others in the group.

Name Collage

Purpose:
This could be a get-acquainted activity. The objective is to give each student an opportunity to think about oneself and to create a simple collage of magazine pictures that describes oneself to others.

Procedure:
1. Give the students some magazines from which they can cut out four or five things that represent them. They can use pictures, advertisements, slogans—anything that tells about who they are at this time in life.

2. Allow approximately 15 to 20 minutes for students to cut out their pictures and then have them paste the cut-outs in a meaningful arrangement on a piece of construction paper.

3. Form small groups and have the students discuss their collages with one another.

The Self-Disclosing Scroll

Purpose:

This activity can be used to evaluate an experience. It can help to foster creativity and abstract thinking.

Procedure:

1. Following the completion of one of the facilitative activities in this book, a curriculum unit, a class project, or whatever, give a small roll of newsprint and some crayons to the students. Tell them to evaluate the activity in terms of "What it meant to me." This will be done through a drawing.

2. Divide the class into four equal groups and then have the members of a group pair off until each student has a number.

3. Have the four No. 1s (drawn from the four groups), four No. 2s, four No. 3s and so forth get together for ten minutes and discuss the completed activity in terms of what it meant to them. They should try to decide on a symbol, picture, words, or whatever, for their drawing. If they cannot decide on one, they may have four different ones or even four different ideas within one symbol.

4. Roll out the newsprint and ask each group of four to stake off an area of the paper and draw their symbol. Poems or limericks may also be used in the drawing.

5. As soon as each group of four has finished with their drawing, hang the papers on the wall at about eye level.

6. Have each group of four explain their evaluation to the rest of the class.

7. Lead the class in a discussion of the experience.

Other Self-Awareness
and Self-Disclosure Activities

Aimlessness

Procedure:
Ask the members of the class to walk aimlessly about the room without talking. Do not give any further instructions. Watch as they divide into subgroups. Which ones tend to seek each other out? Some members will return to their seats quicker than others. Others may be boisterous or more physical, while still others may be quiet. The final class discussion should focus on the group members' tendencies toward security, conforming, confusion, self-consciousness, and other aspects of an unstructured situation.

Feeling Cards

Procedure:
Members of the group write down something about themselves that they cannot tell anyone. Names are not written on the cards. Individuals keep their own cards and tell the group how they feel about what they wrote down rather than revealing it.

Ups and Downs

Procedure:
Have students chart their feelings each day during the same time period (e.g., 3:00 p.m. each day). They should keep the chart for a month and share it with the class.

Developing the Senses

Procedure:
For one day have the students pay particular attention to what their sense of smell reveals about the world around them. They are to list all the odors that they were aware of during the day. Other senses might be explored another day. Finally, after there are lists using all the five senses, a theme might be written utilizing these descriptive words in a story. Students should close their eyes when concentrating on their sensory impressions.

Birth Order

Procedure:
Divide the class into four groups according to birth order. Each group is told to discuss experiences that occur in their lives as a result of sibling position.

Who Am I?

Procedure:
Ask the students to close their eyes and to see what first comes to mind when they ask themselves "Who am I?" The group reports and discusses its responses and then repeats this procedure with the following two questions, each in turn: "Who am I?" and "Who did my parents want me to be?" This experiment can be useful in calling attention to self-identity and parental influences.

Heroes

Procedure:
Have the students tell or write about a significant person that they know, have read about or would like to be like. They are encouraged to elaborate about their heros, including perceived morals and values, lifestyle, and so forth.

Your Most Important Beliefs

Procedure:
Have the individual students list five of their most important beliefs. For each belief make a list of friends who might share it and another list of friends who do not. Check lists by discussing beliefs with friends. Were the original lists accurate?

Have students make a list of the beliefs that they hold today that are "shared" by their parents. Compare this list with another list of beliefs that they hold contrary to those of their parents. Discuss in small groups.

Draw Yourself

Procedure:
Ask students to draw or sketch a picture of their selves. On the back of the same paper, or by creating another picture, have them make a composite of how they think the rest of the class perceives them. When finished, have them compare and discuss the two pictures with others in the class.

After several weeks, repeat the process without referring to the first effort. Compare the two sets of pictures.

Symbolic Objects

Procedure:
Divide into small groups and ask each student to select something (or things) concrete from the environment that symbolizes oneself. Have the students present their objects and describe how they represent them. For example, someone might choose keys for an object and then describe those keys as representing a search for answers, always looking for ways to open doors and truth.

The Grocery Bag

Procedure:
Each student is given a large paper bag. Provide students with crayons, pictorial magazines, and cellophane tape. Students should draw or tape pictures to the outside of the paper bag that they feel best describes them to the others and that they feel safe in sharing. On the inside of the bag they should put pictures of that part of themselves which they do not feel safe in sharing with others. Students may wish to close their bags with staples. Divide the class into small groups for discussion. Do not force students to share the pictures inside their bags. This should be voluntary. You may wish to have students develop their bags at home. Also, themes may be written about the experience.

Clothes with a Meaning

Procedure:
On an assigned day ask students to bring or to wear to class an object or an apparel that represents "how you perceive yourself." Everyone is given an opportunity to try to understand each others' representation. Discuss this activity in terms of what clothes have to say about people, the emphasis upon designer labels, and what about self is revealed or concealed.

How do clothes represent the sign of the times? Trace the recent and past history of clothing. Do clothes reveal more than superficial values? If you could wear any clothes of your own choosing, what would you wear? If you could only wear one set of clothes for the next month for all occasions, what would you wear? If you could select clothes for another person in the class to wear, how would you have that person dress?

Section Five:

Self-Appraisal and Appraisal of Others

- ☐ Positive Appraisal
- ☐ The Application
- ☐ Positive Superlatives
- ☐ Famous Persons
- ☐ Assignment of Famous People
- ☐ New Names and Future Jobs
- ☐ The Trust Walk
- ☐ Expressing Perceptions
- ☐ First Impression

- ☐ Object Assignment
- ☐ Self Metaphors
- ☐ Choosing a Family
- ☐ I Am/You Are
- ☐ The Amnesia Game
- ☐ Descriptions or Metaphors
- ☐ Sculpturing
- ☐ Guess Who

Self-Appraisal

It seems obvious that personal and academic growth are related into the individual's striving to understand oneself better and to assess one's impact on the environment. Unfortunately, too many people equate self-search or self-awareness with a kind of amateur psychoanalytic process where people attempt to interpret their actions and explain why they do the things that they do. Self-appraisal is a self-study. It is taking inventory of one's self. It is an honest and open examination of thoughts, feelings, values, significant events, and influencing factors in one's life.

In a sense, self-appraisal involves a person's taking stock of oneself and saying honestly, "This is who I am," or "This is what I tend to be like, and this is how others tend to see me." Or, "This is what I am becoming and this is what I would like to be." As a consequence of this thinking process, one can gain more insight, take more responsibility, set goals, and do what it takes to accomplish those goals.

Self-appraisal is often thought to be a common part of everyone's everyday life. That is, we think about ourselves throughout the day, mentally talking with ourselves. Sometimes we chastize, and sometimes we praise. Many times, we apply labels to ourselves, based on the value system that we have within ourselves and the conclusions we have reached based on what we have accomplished (We are smart or stupid; strong or weak, good or bad, effective or incompetent). Such value judgments, without exploration of our behaviors and consequences of those behaviors, can be self-defeating. Too often such judgments obscure personal insights, which can be gained by avoiding general labels and focusing on feelings and behaviors that are involved in the experience. Getting a perspective on life is not easy without a systematic self-appraisal of ourselves and the problems that we encounter.

Self-appraisal is more than talking to one's self. As an only means, it is too limited. Our personal defenses come into play and may distort or deny valuable information about ourselves. Therefore, it can be helpful to involve others in the process and encourage them to provide some feedback. They can tell us the kind of impact that our behavior is having on them. They need not judge us as good or bad, as right or wrong... although some cannot resist. Rather, their impressions of what they experience when we do things is the most valuable part.

Some individuals are simply too severe on themselves. Others have mistakenly appraised themselves in one way, only to be confronted by others who see them in a different light. Between a private self-appraisal and a public self-appraisal, that is, in the presence of a group of people, there is an opportunity for persons to learn the most about themselves.

Appraisal of Others

In addition to self-appraisal, a person can be assisted to grow personally and academically when one becomes involved in the active process of helping others appraise themselves. While someone may earnestly request some feedback about oneself for one's own self-appraisal, there is some evidence to suggest those who are participating in the helping process of appraising others also learn something about themselves.

Specifically, when we disclose to others the kind of impact that they seem to have on us or the general picture that we have of them, they learn something about themselves, but we also become more aware of the significance of those people in our life. We do not live in a vacuum. We are affected by the behaviors of others.

As we help others in our lives to think of themselves, we are also saying something about ourselves. And, this information can eventually be a part of our own self-appraisal.

Interestingly enough, when the processes of self-appraisal and appraisal of others are an integrated part of a helping relationship, then all those who are involved tend to feel closer to one another. A stronger trust relationship is formed. The foundation for a more effective working relationship is laid.

The educational process in our schools is concerned with accountability and evaluation. As discussed in Chapter 2, learning is best when it is self-evaluated. But this does not mean that a teacher or group of peers should avoid being a part of the self-evaluation process. Quite the contrary, with their help it is more likely that an individual will gain more insight and achieve more.

The activities in this section are designed to facilitate self-appraisal and the appraisal of others.

Self-Appraisal and Appraisal of Others Activities

Positive Appraisal

Purpose:
To appraise the positive aspects of one's self and to hear positive feedback from others.

Procedure:
1. Lead a discussion concerning the difficulty of describing ourselves to others in a positive manner. You might say something similar to this:

   "We often describe ourselves negatively, putting ourselves down. We have learned to be modest and may even resist describing ourselves in a positive manner, for fear that others might think that we are being conceited or self-centered. We tend to think it is okay to compliment someone else, but can feel rather foolish when we compliment ourselves. Both skills are valuable in our personal growth and development. During this activity we are going to talk about our strengths to other members of the group with the understanding that no one will put us down. It will be an opportunity for you to think aloud about what you like about yourself."

2. Divide the class into small groups consisting of 5-6 members each.

3. Every member in a group writes down at least two positive statements about themselves.

4. Then, members take turns telling their positive strengths to the group.

5. After an individual finishes talking, the group members give that person feedback as to where they agree and where they think the individual missed some strengths. No negative comments are made during this activity.

The Application

Purpose:
This activity is intended to elicit self-disclosure, self-appraisal, and feedback.

Procedure:
1. Give each student a dittoed sheet with the following information on it:

   a. I am applying for the position of:

   b. I feel that I would succeed in this job because:

      1.
      2.
      3.

   c. However, I feel you should also know:

      1.
      2.
      3.

   d. I am anxiously awaiting your reply concerning my future employment.

   Sincerely yours,

2. Students fill out the application for themselves. They may apply for any job that they wish, one that is realistic in the near future or a dream job. Questions or statements on the application can be changed to suit the group's purpose.

3. After each person as filled out the application form, divide the class into small groups and:

   a. Put the forms into a secret pool; draw them out one at a time and have the group guess who wrote the application.

   b. Have each person read one's own application form and obtain feedback from other members in the group.

4. Encourage others in the class to add or delete something from the applicant's form.

Positive Superlatives

Purpose:

To provide positive feedback to students.

Procedure:

1. Divide the class into five groups.

2. Each group uses approximately five minutes to arrive at positive superlatives. That is, members must reach some general consensus that one member in their group is the most "something." For example, four members in a group of five might decide that the fifth member is the friendliest or happiest student. The person to whom the superlative is being applied must not participate in the first part of the discussion. That person only listens.

3. As soon as a positive superlative has been determined for each person in the group, a description tag is pinned on.

4. After each member has a positive superlative pinned on, time is used to give feedback in a go-around. Someone volunteers to hear the other four members speak about why they feel the label or tag is appropriate. In this respect each member provides a supportive statement from one's own experience as to why this person deserves the positive superlative. Giving an example in this matter provides specific data for the person to process. Each member listens to the others speak, and then another person volunteers to receive feedback.

5. The group then discusses how they felt about going through the experience. Some teachers may want to follow up the experience by having students write a theme about their feelings during the experience. Or, the assigned theme might be to evaluate where the group was wrong and where the group was right. Following the small group discussions, the groups might be mixed to share their superlatives and experiences.

Other Appraisal Procedures

Famous Persons

Procedure:
Divide the class into small groups. Individuals are asked to write on a slip of paper the name of a famous person whom they most admire or would most like to be. The person may be living or dead, real or fictional, as long as it is someone famous. The slips of paper are collected. One at a time the famous names are read aloud. After each name is read, the group discusses their positive and negative feelings about the person, and, in the process, attempts are also made to guess who in the group might have selected the "famous person."

Assignment of Famous People

Procedure:
This procedure is related to the famous persons procedure except that in this case the names of famous people are listed on cards. The cards are then placed in the middle of the circle and each one draws a card. That person then tells the group impressions of this famous person. Others help elaborate on the description. Most likely there will be negative and positive comments. After each famous person is described, the task is then to assign the roles to the people in the group. Who is each person most like?

New Names and Future Jobs

Procedure:
Students shed their names and past identities by taking new names and assigning them a future job. Even though the members of the group are familiar with each other, new names and future jobs are assigned as a way of giving feedback.

The Trust Walk

Procedure:
Have the students select a partner and then have one blindfold the other. Without any talking, the guide leads the blindfolded student around the building, helping that person move from place to place. After a while, the students trade places. How long does it take to develop confidence and trust in a person when no words are spoken? What kinds of messages are given and received during the excursion?

This experience can elicit a discussion of trust. it is important for both people to discuss the experience, when they felt trust or reservations. Do they feel more trusting of their partners now? What were some of the feelings they experienced as their guides led them through certain kinds of places?

Expressing Perceptions

Procedure:
Have students select partners in class. Sitting face-to-face with each other, and in turn, they express their perceptions about their partners.

Suggestions:
Describe the other's immediate behavior and appearance. Use no judgmental statements or observations. Simply describe what you see.

Verbalize your feelings about the other's appearance and behavior and about the situation in which you are now. Avoid generalities.

First Impressions

Procedure:
After students have known each other for a period of time, ask each person to write down the first impressions one thinks others have when one meets a group of students. Then ask this person to join with three others to make a group of four. Each person then writes down one's first impressions of the other three in the group. Finally, the papers are compared. What words are similar? What words are different? How many are positive? How many are negative? What behaviors seem to contribute to making these first impressions?

Object Assignment

Procedure:

Students are instructed to sit in a circle. Various objects are placed in the middle of the group. Ask members to give another person in the group one of the objects if they wish. Objects might include: stuffed play snake, hammer, men's slippers, mirror, and a pillow. The object of this game is to elicit personal reactions to giving, receiving, and not being included.

Some variations:

1. Students who are given objects later give them to someone else.

2. All objects are put back in the center and the process is repeated after a time.

3. The people who do not receive any objects are encouraged to tell what they would have expected to receive and from whom. This procedure focuses on four levels of involvement:
   a. receiving
   b. helping
   c. giving and receiving
   d. neither giving nor receiving.

Self-Metaphors

Procedure:

Have the individual students in a group tell how they see themselves as a specific object. They tell why they think of themselves in this way. For example, "If I were a tree, I would be an oak, because it is tall and has strength." After a person speaks, the other members of the class give that person feedback in terms of a) the object that was selected, and b) of a substitute object they have in mind. In this case, the group procedure elicits both self-disclosure and feedback.

I Am/You Are

Procedure:
Divide the class into even-numbered groups and have them pair off within the groups. The pairs should talk to one another for five to ten minutes in order to know each other better. Then, have each member of a dyad write at the top of a piece of paper "I am" and list three adjectives that best describe that person. Then, each student writes at the top of another piece of paper "You are" and lists three adjectives that best describe one's partner. Members of the dyads then exchange papers, return to their small groups, and compare papers. Other group members enter into the discussion.

The Amnesia Game

Procedure:
A student pretends to be suffering from amnesia and doesn't know about oneself. The other students tell things that will give clues as to how the person suffering from amnesia "used to" behave. The person then asks questions of the other members of the class to learn more about oneself. For example, a) How do I act when... (a certain situation)? b) What are my favorite words or expressions? c) How do I act in the classroom or talk with a teacher? Or, as a facilitator, you might pose the questions to the students who are giving feedback.

Descriptions or Metaphors

Procedure:
This procedure encourages analogies or metaphors as part of a feedback process. The basic question is, "What is this person like or of what does the individual remind you?" It is a variation of a popular parlor game in which an individual is likened to something other than a human being. Participants are asked to express their reactions to another person through such questions as, "What kind of tree, food, country, piece of furniture, period of history, or animal would this person be?"

There may be a mix of metaphors when a group is attempting to give an individual feedback. There is no need to arrive at a consensus. That is, group members speak for themselves and from their own experiences with the person. Although an individual might be described as a lion by more than one person, each one will make the lion fit one's own personal reference points and experiences.

Sculpturing

Procedure:
Have a student strike a pose (as if the student was a statue) that depicts a part of one's personality. The rest of the class joins in by voluntarily moving the person to pose in a way as they see that person. Later, a student might sculpt an individual based on one's experiences and then place oneself in the scene—striking one's own pose. This would provide feedback about personal perceptions of an individual and about the perceived relationship.

Discussion following this nonverbal feedback can lead to a more direct feedback process.

Guess Who?

Procedure:
Divide the class into groups. Each group member is asked to write anonymously on a slip of paper three words teachers might use to describe the writer (or, three words one would use to describe oneself). The slips of paper are pooled and then drawn randomly. as each slip of paper is read aloud, the group attempts to guess who wrote the words. Each member who guesses should also give some reason for the speculation. The procedure leads to feedback that is effective for self-appraisal and appraisal of others.

Choosing a Family

Procedure:
The teacher states, "Let us imagine that you could create a family of your own. Chose from among the other students present who you would like to be your mother, father, younger sibling, older sibling, spouse, son, and daughter." Students write down their choices for each category. In a go-around, students report their choices for each category together with some explanations. They then share their observations and reactions with others. What does your pattern of choices suggest about what is important in your life and what you may have missed in your family? Who was most frequently and least frequently chosen for which role? What were your reactions to having or not having been chosen for this or that family role by this or that member or number of members?

Combining Facilitative Responses and Facilitative Procedures

It is not likely that you will use in a single year or with a single class all of the facilitative activities discussed in this and the previous sections. In addition, you will learn about many other activities, some of which you will use and some you will not. You will make up your own activities and modify others. You will discover those that you like and others that simply do not fit your interest or style.

The activities and general procedures in this book were selected to illustrate how a facilitative teacher might use structured learning experiences to help students think about themselves and others. They can also be modified to be incorporated as part of personalizing learning in an academic curriculum.

Of more importance than which or how many procedures are used is the question of the follow-up discussions. Here you will use the facilitative responses discussed in Chapter 3. It may appear to some readers that we put the cart before the horse by placing the facilitative responses before the facilitative activities in this book. Our purpose was intentional, however. Too many teachers have become dependent upon the activities themselves, thinking the procedures alone will accomplish the goals. To the contrary, the activities are only a means to creating opportunities to facilitate student learning and to build positive working relationships.

Conclusion
What Now?

This book has been designed to help you think about facilitative teaching. A few essential skills have been identified and you have had an opportunity to practice them by completing the worksheets. There are, no doubt, other skills and more concepts that might be presented. However, facilitative teachers are also managers— managers of their time, their classrooms, their teaching skills, and the learning process. In addition, being a facilitative teacher means being a self-manager. This requires you to apply the same facilitative principles to yourself—increased self-awareness, self-appraisal, feedback, and personal growth.

As you think about this book, what stands out most in your mind? What did you like least about it? What did you like best? Of all the things that you studied and reviewed, which one has made the most difference in your work with students? Where do you go from here?

Research and the practical experience of successful teachers continues to emphasize that personal relationships are the heart of teaching. Teaching can be for better or for worse. As a facilitative teacher, you can make a positive difference with students and be a credit to yourself and the teaching profession.

References

Amidon, E., & Giammatteo, M. (1967). The verbal behavior of superior elementary teachers. In E. Amidon & J. Hough, *Interaction analysis: Theory research and application.* Reading, MA: Addison-Wesley Publishing Co.

Barr, A.S. (1929). *Characteristic differences in the teaching performance of good and poor teachers of the social studies.* Bloomington, IL: Public School Publishing Co.

Brammer, L. M. (1988). *The helping relationship: Process and skills.* Englewood Cliffs, NJ: Prentice Hall.

Cohan, M. L. (1958). The relation of the behavior of teachers to the productive behavior of their pupils. *Journal of Experimental Education, 27,* 89-124.

Cruickshank, D.R. (1986). Profile of an effective teacher, *Educational Horizons, 64,* 80-86.

Cunningham, R. (1988). Make kindling of those school hickory sticks, *Gainesville Sun* (Editoral), January 23. Gainesville, FL.

Ellena, W.J. Stevenson, M; & Webb, H.F. (1961). *Who's a good teacher?* Washington, DC: American Association of School Administrations, NEA.

Emmerling, F.C. (1961). A study of the relationships between personality characteristics of classroom teachers and pupil perception. Unpublished Doctoral Dissertation, Auburn, AL: Auburn University.

Faust, V. (1968). *The Counselor-consultant in the elementary school.* Boston: Houghton Mifflin.

Gallop, G.H. (1988). Gallop poll public opinion, 1986-1988. Wilmington, DE: S.R. Scholarly Resources, Inc.

Getting tough. (1988). *Time Magazine, 131* (5), 52-58.

Guddemi, M., Swick, K., & Brown, M. (1987). Personality dimensions of prospective teachers: A critical analysis. *Teacher Educator, 22,* 2-7.

Gurney, P. (1987). Self-esteem enhancement in children: a review of research findings. *Educational Research, 29,* 130-136.

Martin, A. (1987). Encouraging youngsters to discuss their feelings, *Learning, 6,* 80-81.

Maslow, A.H. (1962). *Toward a psychology of being.* New York: Van Nostrand.

Maslow, A.H. (1954). *Motivation and personality.* New York: Harper & Row.

Morsh, J.E., & Wilder, E.W. (1954). Identifying the effective instructor: A review of quantitative studies 1900-1952. *Research Bulletin,* Lackland Air Force Base, TX: Air Force Personnel and Training Center, October.

Myrick, R.D. (1987). *Developmental guidance and counseling: A practical approach.* Minneapolis, MN: Educational Media Corporation.

Pfeiffer, J.W., & Jones, J.E. (1971-1979). *A handbook of structured experiences for human relations training, seven volumes.* La Jolla, CA: University Associates.

Purkey, W.W., & Novak, J.M. (1988). *Education: By invitation only.* Bloomington, IN: Phi Delta Kappa Educational Foundation.

Replogle, B.L. What help do teachers want? (1950). *Educational Leadership, 7,* 445-449.

Rogers, D. & Waller, C. & Perrin, M. (1987). Learning what makes a good teacher good through collaborative research in the classroom. *Young Children, 42,* 34-39.

Appendix

(Answers to Worksheets 1 - 6)

Worksheet 1—Possible Answers

(Our Feeling-Focused Responses)

The following are possible reflecting/understanding responses to student statements found on worksheet 1.

Example A:
"You're disappointed that you won't be in the advanced group."

Example B:
"You're upset and frustrated with your parents."

Example C:
"You're proud of yourself."

Example D:
"You enjoyed the break from school, but you're feeling uneasy about coming back."

Worksheet 2—Possible Answers
(Clarifying/Summarizing Responses)

Example A:

"Traveling would be one way to meet new friends."

Example B:

"You find biology lab disturbing."

Example C:

"You're wondering if you are ever going to catch up."

Worksheet 3—Possible Answers
(Some Open-Ended Responses)

Example 1:
"What was it about reading that kept you from working harder?"

Example 2:
"What is it about math that you find most difficult?"

Example 3:
"When do you find yourself being the most scared?"

Worksheet 4—Possible Responses

Student 1:

Type of response given: Reflecting feeling

Example of open-ended question: "What were your expectations?"

Student 2:

Type of response given: Reassurance/support

Example of clarifying response: "The test results verified your future plans and you're wondering if you'll be successful at accounting."

Student 3:

Type of response given: Clarification/summarizing

Example of open-ended question: "What type of questions cause you to feel this way?"

Student 4:

Type of response given: Interpretation/analysis

Example of reflecting response: That comment angered you.

Student 5:

Type of response given: Advice

Example of clarifying response: "You've having difficult with what I'm saying."

Student 6:

Type of response given: Advice

Example of reflecting response: "It's confusing to you."

Worksheet 5—Possible Responses

Pairing Responses

Students 1 and 2:
Example of pairing response: "You both were stimulated and enjoyed that part of the exercise."

Students 3 and 4:
Example of pairing response: "You two are different in what satisfies you. John, you want to lead others and, Jim, that's not something you would like to do."

Students 5 and 6:
Example of pairing response: "You both want to use some of the money as an investment."

Simple Acknowledgement Responses

Case 1:
"Okay, Sara, now let's think some more about Egypt."

Case 2:
"Alright, Hassan, ...but first let's make sure that we understand what John is saying." (Turn back to John and continue).

Worksheet 6—Possible Feedback Responses

1. I noticed that you (group of students) were working quietly at the activity center while I was busy with Mr. Jamison. I am appreciative. It makes me want to tell others what hard workers you are.

2. When I saw you walking quietly from the library, it made me feel proud of you for being so thoughtful and I just wanted to let you know that before we started today.

3. You know, class, when you continued to work, even though I was busy with our visitor, I experienced a lot of pride... and relief. I was able to concentrate on our visitor's questions.

4. When you (students) don't participate, but interrupt our activities, it's irritating. It makes me want to send you back to the classroom.

5. Flinging the paper around may be fun for you; however, it annoys me and that makes me want to ask you to leave the class.